MORE
LETTERS FROM LONGSTOCK

ILLUSTRATED BY GRAHAM HUMPHRIES

Also by Geoffrey Snagge
LETTERS FROM LONGSTOCK

Geoffrey Snagge

MORE LETTERS FROM LONGSTOCK

PELHAM BOOKS

To the mother of
Sophia, Lucy and Mary Jane

7207 0457 X

Set and printed in Great Britain by Tonbridge Printers Ltd, Peach Hall Works, Tonbridge, Kent, in Bell eleven on thirteen point, on paper supplied by P. F. Bingham Ltd, and bound by James Burn at Esher, Surrey

1967

Back from Foreign Parts

25th November

A short time ago we had the good fortune to be given the chance to visit friends in America and Canada, a chance, of course, that we seized with both hands, so that there has had to be a break in these letters.

In the course of a journey such as we made, travelling all the way on sea and land, one sees great wonders. The vast mountains and forests of the Rockies; the turquoise blue Lake Louise sparkling in the sun against its brilliant background of snow and glacier; great whales spouting their salty plumes off the coast of Newfoundland; the quick smooth efficiency of the passage through the Panama Canal and then the continuous rumbling of the waves rolling in on the western coast for hundreds and hundreds of miles with every now and again the sound of seals barking on the rocks just beyond where the long great seas crash and hiss ashore.

Twice we saw the deep red sun sink below the Pacific horizon leaving a sky of every colour one knows, with here and there a shade that one seemed never to have seen before. Another of our permanent memories will be the soft tropical nights at sea and one especially when for full measure a man-made satellite came hurrying across the sky busy about its scientific experiments, which seemed trivial against the back-

7

ground of Orion and the great shining galaxies that lay beyond.

Many other sights and experiences crowd into one's mind as one thinks of those weeks, but it is all too close yet to single out any particular one as being more impressive than another, though as these memories pile in all jumbled up I think my wife and I both find that the one that turns up most often is our journey through the Red Wood Forests on the West Coast.

I doubt if anyone can convey in words, painting, music, or any other means of communication, the feeling that walking in these forests can give to one. The sheer size of the trees is overwhelming and one feels that if you were to shout as loud as you could it would only come out a silly little muffled squeak. I have heard it said that to walk among these huge trees gives people a sense of inferiority and insignificance. I do not think this is so. Certainly it was not our experience. Rather it was that one felt one became some tiny part of it all and had a comfortable feeling of security and peace as if some great kindly Power was very near and knew that we were both there.

However all that may be, it is not the part of these letters to try and express one's personal feelings of this sort but to try and pass on the more ordinary experiences of living in our small community and so provide those readers to whom it may be of interest with a few minutes' respite from the useful and busy clamour of their city lives.

We only got back a day or two ago. We arrived in the late afternoon of a cold calm cloudy day. The garden had a mournful look with plants lying dead and dying among foot-high weeds in every bed. Brown wet leaves covered the lawn. The rain dripped steadily from the thatch as I fumbled for the key, but we were home.

The Last of the Leaves

Almost the whole of one's time this last fortnight seems to have been spent sweeping up leaves. It has been a bad year for leaf-sweepers. There have been no severe frosts and no gales to bring the leaves down in one go; they have just trickled down gently and steadily all day and all night for weeks. You leave them until you cannot bear it any longer and then spend a boring two or three hours sweeping them up, and a day or two later you have to do it all over again when it seems to take twice as long. But it looks as if it is at last done, the trees are now bare, the last stray vestige of colour on any dying plant has gone and we have settled down to face the long haul of the winter to come.

We have as usual a robin who takes a great interest in all our doings and even sweeping leaves seems to interest him, though he too gets bored with it after a short time, but he comes back every twenty minutes or so to see if there are any pickings. I do not know if he is the same one that we got to know so well last winter. Having been away for so long one gets out of touch and in any case during the summer we do not see much of each other. In a few weeks' time when the weather turns really cold and I shall be doing a bit of digging we will no doubt get to know each other better.

I have come to the conclusion that at this time of year when the ground is still soft and seeds plentiful it must be curiosity rather than cupboard love that makes him and others appear so friendly. Last week I had to cut off a big broken branch that was hanging down from a tree. It was the height of a two-span ladder some twenty feet or more from the ground and as I was sawing away he flew up and sat on a branch quite close to watch me do it. He must have known that at that height there was little chance of my turning up any tit-bits. A day or two later I was setting a mole trap in a desperate attempt to catch one of the little brutes that was ruining the lawn and as soon as I had finished he flew down and perched on the trap itself to have a closer look at what I had been up to.

Needless to say I had no success with the trap and the next morning not only was it sprung but it was half buried under one of the half dozen or so mole hills that had been made during the night.

One of the lessons in Church last Sunday was from Isaiah when, if I heard aright, he prophesied that on the Day of Judgement, among other worrying things that would happen, men would cast their silver and gold to the moles and the bats. I am ashamed to admit that as soon as I heard these words I resolved there and then that no matter how great the general disturbance and even if it were the last thing that I ever did, I would make absolutely certain that not one piece of my silver – no not even one small solitary salt spoon – would be cast to a mole. *Every single bit* would be cast to a bat.

Christmas Time Comes to Longstock

'So let the organ thunder
While choirs with peals of glee
Do rend the air asunder.'

So runs part of an old English carol that we sang in our carol service last Sunday. While perhaps our efforts fell a little short of what the carolist had in mind when he wrote these words a good many years ago, they were not far off.

This year, Mr Tewkesbury, who is a member of the Winchester Cathedral choir, brought a party of volunteers to sing some seasonal church music unaccompanied which, as might be expected from so talented a party, they did beautifully. Young sidesmen and sideswomen (if there are such things in the church hierarchy), whose ages range from six to sixteen, also, for the first time, sang a carol on their own. In spite of the bitterly cold night the church was almost full, so when we all got going together on the more familiar hymns such as *Hark the Herald Angels Sing*, with Miss Child pulling out as many stops as possible on the organ and playing with all hands and feet, the air was pretty well rent asunder if not quite. Anyway whether it was or not matters little as we all felt the better for letting ourselves go and congratulated ourselves in the porch afterwards.

Tomorrow the over 60's hold their party in the Village Hall where there is to be a conjuror. Mr Fudge has lit up the tree in his garden with coloured lights and so Christmas time has once more come to Longstock.

It is indeed welcome. We need a little cheering up for it has been a strange fortnight. We had intense cold which caught us all on the hop, and a blizzard so thick that at one moment one could not see more than five yards ahead for quite a long time. This made getting about difficult and in some nearby areas impossible. This was followed by an almost sultry spell and today we are back to flurries of powdery snow and biting cold. So much so that when I was trying to wash off some of the thick mud that the car had collected during the thaw the water froze solid and covered the car with dirty ice like icing on a coffee cake.

The cold spell brought an unwelcome visit of a rat into our drawing room through a large hole that he had made in the carpeted floor. He also chewed large hunks out of it in his efforts to get out under the door. He must have found some other way because my wife met him the next evening in semi-darkness in the hall where they both frightened each other very much but, whereas my wife bravely stood her ground, the rat bolted. I do not wish to be misunderstood but I wish that it had been the other way round. My wife could not have bolted further than the kitchen because I had locked up, but heaven knows where the rat has bolted to for I cannot find him any-where. I hope he has not died of shock or, if he has, that it was sufficiently delayed until he got outside.

1968

Flower of Promise

It is perhaps appropriate that today, New Year's Day, we should find our first snowdrop fully out. Actually I think she has been out for a day or two as there are two others still in bud poking up alongside her. But I have not been that way since last I went mole-catching a few days ago.

In these times, when all the experts and Dismal Jimmies are predicting the difficulties and miseries that the year holds in store for us all, it is a comfort to find such a certain sign of something very pleasant to come. One knows, of course, perfectly well that the snowdrops will never fail, but nevertheless the sight of the first one cheers one up and gives one confidence that, even if the experts are right, the miseries and difficulties can be but temporary against the unconquerable background of the general order of things.

Snowdrops have, of course, been out here for some days now and the small clump under the Gingko tree in the churchyard was as usual on duty to welcome churchgoers on Christmas morning. Mrs Mason, who was born in this village, told me that she has seen them there on Christmas Day almost as far back as she can remember, so our own little plantation, to which we try to add each year, should see us out.

We have so far, in spite of quite reasonable weather, been

unable to catch up on the two months during which we were away from the garden. In an attempt to try to do so we decided that it was high time to replant the spring bulbs that we had dug up last summer, only to find that not only had the mice eaten the lot but had also taken the whole bottom of the sack in which they were stowed to build themselves very warm and cosy nests within easy walking distance of their newly-found supermarket. The irritation caused by the discovery was for a moment or two beyond measure because I realised that it was entirely my own fault in not slinging the sack up out of the way of temptation; but this was soon tempered by the realisation that a back-aching job could now be wiped off the list of arrears with no more effort than a stroke of a pencil. Nevertheless it did seem a little ungrateful of the mice after we had so consistently fed them on crocus bulbs besides a very liberal allowance of sweet peas from the greenhouse.

Today there is no chance of putting to the test our New Year resolution to get the garden up to date, for it is foggy and cold with a drizzle melting the slushy snow that fell in the night. Even the birds waiting for the bird table to be replenished sit with their feathers fluffed out, looking damp and miserable, as if they had just finished reading the prognostications of the experts. It is time they flew down to the bottom of the garden and had a look at the snowdrop. It would do them all good.

The Turn of the Year

20th January

One of the many things that have mystified me for a long time is the curious feeling that comes, I think, to all of us quite suddenly and unexpectedly that the year has turned. I felt it this week and I do not remember having felt it so early in the year before. It lasted only a few seconds but there was no doubt about it and one felt the gooseflesh run down one's spine as sometimes it does when listening to a certain bit of music or reading a line or two of poetry or perhaps just looking at something very beautiful.

I tried to find the reason for it but was quite unable to do so. It happened on a dull cold morning typical of any winter's day. I was indoors lazily reading rather a dull article in the morning paper and feeling rather bored as an attack of flu was preventing me from going out. No birds were singing, no sun was shining, and I was not even looking out of the window, and yet suddenly I felt the change and knew that the year had begun again. Lots of people have told me that they have the same experience so it is not imagination on my part; but, whatever the reason, it is a remarkably pleasant feeling and all the more welcome perhaps because as one gets older one tends, I suppose, to get less sensitive and so pleasurable emotions become more rare.

I have mentioned before in these letters that we have a small bird table on the window sill of our bedroom. It has always

been fun to have, but a day or two in bed made me realise what a tremendous boon such a bird table could be to those un-fortunate people who have to spend much of their time, or possibly all of it, in bed. I imagine it would be worth while almost anywhere and even if it were only used by a few house sparrows each bird seems to have his own tricks and mannerisms which are fascinating to watch and in a very short time one can recognise one from another. Anyway I pass on the idea, for what it may be worth, to any who have invalid friends or relations. It costs almost nothing to make and needs only a few scraps to maintain.

Having been confined to barracks I am unable to report on progress outside, though no doubt there has been plenty going on even at this time of year. A small drake has been visiting us fairly often. We have called him Francis for want of a better name as I cannot recognise him from my small bird book. I think he may belong to Mr Terry Jones' duckery for he is much tamer than the mallards who visit us and whom one cannot ever get near at all. We have been putting down some barley every morning to encourage him but he seems to have gone off again. However, it has been worth while as there are plenty of other customers who come for it and who are nice to have around, such as a pheasant or two and ducks and wood pigeons. None very helpful in the garden but at this time of year they can't do much harm, and anyway you cannot have it all your own way all the time.

Moles on the Rampage

3rd February

While I was laid up in bed the moles rampaged down the whole length of our new herbaceous border, tearing at its edges and uprooting many plants, and then broke out into the lawn beyond and threw up about a dozen molehills within a patch about five yards square, ruining that piece of lawn for months to come unless I can find time to dig it up and relay the turf.

It is an extraordinary thing that, although I have many friends and acquaintances who are keen on gardening, a number of whom are admittedly a little odd if not to say peculiar, I cannot call to mind even one who one could truthfully describe as stark staring bonkers and I cannot understand why. I just do not believe that I alone, among all those many friends and acquaintances, am the only one who suffers from moles, nor do I believe that my nervous system is less robust than those of some of the twittering old dears with whom I have talked about gardening. I suppose what really happens is that those who finally succumb are put away quietly without anyone knowing the real reason.

We have not seen our friend the little drake for some time but Mr Mott, who knows all there is to know about everybody who lives on or in the river and on the banks fifty yards either side of it, told me this week that he has not gone away and is still with us in the reeds on the other side of our carrier. Mr Mott also told me that I was right in thinking that he came from the duckery and that he is a cross breed, which is why I could not find him in the book.

On the 23rd January, which was a lovely warm sunny day here, I heard a chiffchaff. An ornithological friend of mine gave me an unbelieving look when I told him, but a chiffchaff is unmistakable. I imagine that he must be one who decided to back Britain and not winter abroad this year. Mr Griffiths, who came to live in the village last year and has already done a lot

19

of interesting work in recording our local birds, told me that the first time that he heard one last year was on the 11th March.

Another thing that I was told this week, which may interest those keen on birds, is that about a mile down the road from here there are a lot of bramblings among the beech trees. Dr Johnson, who told me this, said that he had never seen them here before.

Snowdrops are beginning to be out in numbers and daffodils are starting to push through the grass all over the place so one feels that one has only to stick it out a bit longer before things take a turn for the better. It will be a stern two months, however, as February and March are the months when the moles are on the run and when the fields and meadows sprout molehills everywhere. No wonder the hares who live in the fields go a bit dotty in March, poor little dévils.

Death of a Little Drake

Two friends have been kind enough to suggest how to cope with moles in the garden and rats in the house. One of the suggestions – namely that Euphorbia plants will keep moles away – I am afraid I have lost faith in. I tried it fairly extensively two or three years back and for a time believed that there might be something in it but have now decided that there is not. Euphorbia plants now sprout up all over the garden in the most unexpected places from seeds self sown by those I deliberately planted but the moles burrow busily all round them.

Dr Johnson, who is also plagued by moles, tells me that he

has also tried it and found that it did not work. It seems that our local breed of mole is not Euphorbiaphobic, which frankly surprises me as I could believe anything that sounds like that about them.

To stop rats in the house the suggestion was to pour tar and cement into the rat hole. My wife is a tolerant woman and I have had cause to be grateful for her patience on many and all sorts of occasions, but I am reasonably certain that if I were to be discovered carrying buckets of tar and cement into the drawing room I would have reason to believe that I had pushed my luck a bit too far. Nevertheless I am grateful for the suggestion and am bearing it in mind in case our rat should ever return.

We were saddened last week when Mr Burtenshaw told me that there was a dead duck in the undergrowth at the bottom of the garden. I went down to have a look and there lay the little drake whom I have mentioned in these letters and whom we had not seen for some time. He had been dead for quite a while so that my autopsy was perfunctory. Unlike the pigeon, whose feathers and remains I found scattered over quite a wide area in our front garden last week, he had not been caught napping by the cat that comes round here occasionally and there were no obvious signs of a wound. He had been pinioned at one time so Mr Mott was certainly right in telling me that he had come from the duckery. The water meadows have been shot over recently so it is possible that he may have been wounded and managed to make his way back to where he knew he could get a meal without working for it too hard and died of wounds.

On the other hand he may have been just beaten up by the two pairs of mallards who have also discovered that barley is provided gratis round here. After all he was small and on his own and, being a cross breed, he looked a bit funny and he could not fly very well; and the water meadows, like other places in the world to judge from some of the photographs we see these days in the press, are no places for the weak. But he was a nice little chap to have around and we are sorry.

There are two yellow crocuses coming out on our bank so with luck the mice may have overlooked some of the hundreds that we have planted there over the last few years. Mr Sainsbury, who has worked on the land all his long life, and whose great interests throughout those many years have been poetry and local wild life, told me this week that he has never known mice and voles do so much damage. They have even eaten his shallots and onions, a thing he has never known before.

Another friend who has a big garden fairly near here has told me a similar tale. He puts it down to the pesticides and weed-killers used since farming has become big business, with the result that there are not enough insects and seeds left for the birds and other small fry who usually live in the fields and who now have to concentrate on people's gardens. Although this theory is hotly denied by some it seems a reasonable explanation.

Carollers and Crocuses

3rd March

Just before the cold spell set in I heard for the first time this year a serious attempt being made to persuade us all that spring is nearly here. It was by a song thrush perched high up in the elm tree alongside our house. He was standing on the same branch and even the same bit of branch from which someone sang to us all last spring. He must be the same bird, a splendid chap who used to sing not only in the early mornings and when the sun was going down but pretty well all day long. One sometimes wondered how he had the breath to do it.

Experts tell us that the reason why a bird sings is to proclaim his territorial rights and warn off trespassers, but there are a few romantics who say it is to keep the hen happy and amused while she is patiently carrying out the boring chore of hatching out a family. Much as most of us would like to believe this, I cannot bring myself to think that there is much in it. It was impossible to see up there any nest when the leaves were out, but even now when the tree is bare I can see no sign of an old one, though I found one much lower down not thirty yards away.

I really believe that this chap sings away just for the fun of it, as would most of us if we perched near the top of a tree overlooking a lovely valley on a warm spring day and were able to make so beautiful and loud a noise. We are, of course, delighted that he survived the winter and is still with us.

I read somewhere this week that birds have dialects like people and that a good ornithologist can tell from what part of the country a bird comes by the way he sings his song, a snippet of information that I found quite fascinating. I am glad that our thrush has a Hampshire accent – one of the prettiest accents in England, though alas now beginning to die out.

Yesterday a neighbour gave me what sounds a very good tip for preventing mice digging up crocus bulbs. It was to put a pinch of flaked naphthalene in the hole when planting the bulb. The theory is that mice must find the bulbs by smell and that the naphthalene should effectively drown the smell of the crocus bulb. The only catch in it that I can see is that once the mice discover that a smell of naphthalene means a crocus bulb the lot will go in a night.

One could, of course, foil them by planting, say, six blank flakes of naphthalene to every one with a crocus bulb, but I feel that it would be I who would crack before all but the weakest minded mouse. The thought of spending back-breaking hours planting five hundred crocus bulbs fills me with depression, but the thought of planting three thousand individual pieces of barren naphthalene fills me with as much Cimmerian gloom as if I were a moth. Sometimes in the very early hours of the morning, when it is said that the human system is at its lowest ebb, I wake and wonder whether mice are not right and that the sight of crocuses in the spring is not all that it is cracked up to be, but I am glad to say that the mood passes and I realise that perhaps after all mice don't know everything.

Spring Song

We were away five days last week and it brought home to us how much can happen to a garden in five days at this time of year. Admittedly they were five sunny days and some of them fairly warm, but even allowing for all that the difference is extraordinary.

It was a very salutary warning, as watching things day by day, and in our case almost hourly, one does not notice how much progress is being made and how quickly time is slipping by. It is obviously high time that I started overhauling the mowing machine, painting the greenhouse, getting the beds ready and all the other dozens of things that I ought to have been doing during the last few months.

We got back in the evening and, before we went into the house, walked round the garden – and perhaps the first thing we noticed was the birds singing away as if there had been no winter. When we left them five days before there were only one or two optimists who thought it was time to celebrate the turn of the year but now almost all are having a go. Soon no doubt they will be joined by those who have wintered abroad but they cannot ring so true as those who stayed behind with us and stuck it out.

The daffodil buds are beginning to fatten and what few crocuses the mice have left are shining in the sun while the snowdrops begin to fade. These last have not been good this year, I don't know why. Last year we had small thick patches of white in a number of places, but this year there has been nothing like the show and I am wondering whether it is because last year I cut them too soon. Experts say that cutting them down as soon as they have flowered does not matter, but I shall not risk it again.

Bad weather will no doubt return but there can now be no doubt that the grip of winter is loosening fast and very soon now we will once more be congratulating each other on the way things are coming on, as if it had anything to do with us.

We saw a delightful little incident this morning as we stopped on the Bunny bridge, as we often do to see what is going on in the world. There were two swans in the pool below,

looking very beautiful and swimming slowly about, in bright sunshine. Neither was doing very much – other than feeding in a leisurely way – but while we were watching the pen went over to the cob and rubbed her cheek against his and then swam back and went on quietly feeding again. I suppose it should be described as an ornithological courting display, but I am not ashamed to admit that I am a big enough sentimentalist to think that she did it just because she loved him, and the sight has helped to make our day.

A Note of Frustration

31st March

So far this year the weather has gone by the book. A cold snowy January, a dry February and now March gales. If it continues next month with warm April showers we shall all be on the pig's back despite devaluations, escalations, strikes, taxes, index figures, norms, sub norms, politicians, protest meetings and moles.

Although things look little changed from a month ago, there is a tense feeling of expectancy about and we seem to be teetering on the brink of the explosion when nature finally breaks through the crust of winter and once more spills her splendour over the countryside.

Our daffodils, which have multiplied in the last few years to an extent that we can almost say that they are massed, show a yellowish tinge of green and it only needs a couple of warm sunny days to bring them all out at once. We are told that the time has come when we should dig them all up and separate them but, although they are now getting very much smaller, they look very pretty in solid clumps and one wonders whether all the hard work that digging them up and separating them and then replanting them all would entail would really be worth the result.

We have decided to answer the budget by growing our own vegetables. Hitherto it has hardly seemed worth while and we have preferred to use the small space available for growing flowers for the house and for giving to friends who come from London to stay. Neither my wife nor I know much about vegetable growing, so apart from anything else it will be an interesting experiment.

We have already put down a row of peas, which should just fill the hungry gap for mice between their finishing the crocus bulbs and starting on the strawberry season. I understand that pheasants are quite partial to young peas too so we have sown a whole four-ounce packet which should be enough for everybody including ourselves. We have also sown some cabbages and cauliflowers but we are not quite certain yet for whom, other than the caterpillars. Neither of us cares for carrots very much so the slugs and beetles will jolly well have to go without them too and just go on living on a dreary diet of delphinium shoots. Runner beans we have grown now for three years so consider ourselves experts, if not as bean cultivators at any rate as black fly exterminators.

These notes may, I fear, seem a bit depressing but I have just got back from pruning our largest and almost our favourite rose tree, a Danse de Feu, a magnificent and prolific grower but which has easily the largest and sharpest thorns of any in the garden. Somehow or other, I cannot imagine how, I managed to get a long branch up each trouser leg at the same time. I have never had a rose branch up my trouser leg before, though I remember a friend telling me that he had done so once and warning me to take every precaution to see that I never did the same. But, he went on, if by some unlucky chance I ever did then I was to remember not to panic but to sit down quietly and very slowly take my trousers off. It was, he said, the only way. I remembered it all right, but our rose tree is on the public highway and, in any case, with a rose branch up each trouser leg one is completely immobilised and cannot move at all. I don't think I have ever experienced so much frustration, and I apologise to readers if it has shown itself in this letter; I hope they will understand and make allowances.

Number Crunchers and Fossils

On some programme on the television the other day it was said that it was possible that in a few years' time there would be built a computer to which all the great brains of the world would contribute so that it would contain everything important that is known about anything. Presumably therefore, it would not only be able to answer any question but would help people make new discoveries and think new thoughts and hold new theories about things of which at present we have only the dimmest knowledge. It is an idea that ordinary people find difficult to hoist in and is probably best left to leading scientists and philosophers to cope with. For most of us there seems to be quite enough to discover and learn about lying immediately under our noses without having to bother a computer.

This was brought home to me very vividly this week by Mr Gowan Ditchburn, a local bricklayer, who came to mend a small brick wall in the garden. He or his mate, Mr Rolfe, I forget who, suggested that as we had a good many flints lying about it would be cheaper and look nice to include some patterns in the wall. Accordingly, while waiting for the van to take them home, they amused themselves breaking suitable flints into suitable shapes to put in the wall.

I was watching them do it when Mr Ditchburn picked up a long thin flint like a small french loaf which he told me used to be called a 'rag' and was used in the old days to bind flint walls together and could be found in any walls of an old church or building in which flints were used. I remarked that the one he was holding looked like a fish and he astonished me by saying that of course it did because it might have been a fish once. He then pointed out the joints in the spine and where the back fin had been and then breaking it in half showed me the section of the spine itself, all stone of course but the round section of the spine a deeper colour and quite distinct. He said that they were quite common and seeing that I was interested showed me several other fossils that he had found among our flints, two of which had obviously been fairly large cockles and which he said were known locally as Shepherds' Caps. The next morning he showed me another. It was a small brown stone about one and a half inches in diameter broken in half, and in the middle of it, as if it were a little seal, only convex instead of indented, was a perfect little squid with five tentacles, like a tiny hand. One wondered how many millions of years ago this little squid and the cockles and fish were swimming about in our garden. Perhaps it will be something to ask the new computer or number cruncher, as I have heard computers irreverently called.

Someone has been eating our seedling lettuces in the greenhouse at night. I suspected a mouse, but since I caught a shrew in the mouse trap alongside the lettuces a few days ago no more have been eaten, so he may have been the villain. I believe shrews are supposed to eat only insects but I dare say they like a bit of salad with them now and again.

Why have shrews such tiny eyes? They are obviously not made for night work and I should have thought that they were not much use during the day. I suppose a shrew's long nose makes up for poor sight. Anyway it will be another question for the number cruncher.

No sign of the cuckoo or house martin yet and I am not surprised. I should think that if they were on their way here they headed straight back when they realised the bitterly cold weather they would have to face.

Martins, Moorhens and Mouse Traps

The cuckoo has arrived after all. Mr Maurice Jones, the Managing Director of the Leckford Estate, told me that he heard him on 13th April and with him came soft rain and warm sun and we all felt the better for it.

I myself did not hear him until the next day which was, appropriately enough, Easter Sunday. He was a long way off, over on the Leckford side of the valley, chiming in with the distant sound of church bells as if confirming as best he could the great message of hope and of better things to come that the bells were calling out across the valley.

A few days later the house martins arrived and seemed to be in a great state of fuss to find that since they left last year our house has been repainted and thus was destroyed all traces of their old nests; but although the excitement of being home again has died down, and they have for the present it seems lost all interest in the house, I hope they will start building again and not desert us.

Another big event has been the moorhen, which has built her nest in the middle of our carrier in full view of everybody. It had been left alone for at least a week and I thought it was a false nest, but she has now started laying her eggs in it. I can only just see the tops of them so cannot tell how many and do not like to wade out and have a look because, although she may not be there, she is never very far away and I do not wish to frighten her now that she is tame enough to build where she has. Last year she (if she is the same bird) built her nest in the reeds a few feet away from where she has done so now but it was so carefully hidden that I almost trod on it before I saw it.

Our efforts to beat the Budget by growing our own vegetables have been somewhat sabotaged by mice, who have eaten pretty well a whole row of peas. This is most unfair as we sowed enough for everybody, but the mice go and dig things up before anyone else gets a chance. I set traps – but it looks as if the mice are winning in spite of fairly heavy casualties. Gardening round here is more of a blood sport than a hobby.

Yesterday one of the traps was missing. I was wondering who had pinched it or whether a rat had gone off with it round his leg or whiskers when I saw it some four or five yards away, upside down under the hedge. I found that, in spite of the wire netting cage specially put over the peas to prevent it doing so, it had caught a sparrow. The mouse trap was the ordinary break-back kind and had caught the sparrow across the neck

just as if it had been a mouse. The sparrow was still alive and when I released him he flew away out of sight as if nothing had happened. I suppose a bird's neck is made differently from that of a mouse which is always killed instantly or it may be that the feathers protect it; but I would have never believed it possible that a sparrow could get away with it like that had I not seen it for myself.

The Rail Call

The cherry trees are at their best and, to judge by the amount of traffic there is up and down our small road on a fine evening, I suspect that many people from round about motor over specially to see them.

I had the luck to see three of them last week, looking as beautiful as they could be. They are in the little War Memorial garden at the end of the Bunny, the small lane that goes over the river. The three trees, which seemed to be made of solid rose-pink blossom, shone magnificently in the light of the bright sun. In front of them stood the tall pale grey Maltese cross of the memorial itself, while behind them was a great dark purple thunder cloud coming up from the West. The colouring itself made a wonderful picture but the mixture of the tremendous power of the thunder cloud and the fragile delicacy of the blossom made it all something more than a lovely sight.

The recent rains raised the level of the river an inch or two and swamped the moorhen's nest in our carrier, sweeping away the eggs. Nothing daunted, she started yesterday building another about twenty yards further down, also in the middle of the carrier, on another shallow patch where, if the river rises again, exactly the same thing is bound to happen. A bird's I.Q. is well known to be minimal but it must be a bore to be as silly as all that. The nest is even more casually made than her last, as if she thought it hardly worth while making; just a few bits of reed chucked together with a dent in the middle. It looks only half finished but this morning I noticed there is one egg in it so I suppose it is all she is going to do. She is a bit astern of station as last week I came across the nest of another in the reeds on the main river with six eggs, two of which had already hatched out into funny little black creatures with green eyelids and red and yellow beaks, which looked much too big for their tiny frames.

This week I came across someone who I had not seen before in our garden, a brown bird about the size of a large thrush with a long thin head and beak. I only caught a glimpse of him before he dashed off into the reeds. Mr Griffiths told me he thought that he was probably a rail and that I was lucky to see him as they are very shy. There are, it seems, quite a number about as Mr Mott told him that he often hears them down by the river in the early morning. Not knowing what I ought to listen for I looked it up in my little book and it was as well that I did as the author described the rail's call as a 'whitz' and an 'explosive scream or groan'. If I had not read that and had woken up early one morning and had heard it I would probably have telephoned Police Sergeant Hatcher and then retired under the bed clothes to think out whether I should go down and help or not.

Mention of early-morning bird calls reminds me that Mr Lister, the Longstock keeper, told me that he and his wife heard the cuckoo this year for the first time at half past six in the morning on the 9th April. This is the winner so far as I have been told.

Nesting Time

20th May

The river is very low for this time of year in spite of quite a lot of rain recently and the moorhen who built a new nest after her last one had been swept away seems to be getting away with it. She herself seems to have enough confidence to add considerably to the number of reeds that make the nest so that it is now quite a big affair. She is now concentrating on the serious business of hatching her clutch of six eggs and I can pass within a couple of yards of her without her minding, provided that I go fairly quietly. Unlike the nearby blackbird who gets panic stricken and flies off her nest whenever I pass her and remains running about the field clinking her protest until I have gone away.

There is no accounting for tastes when it comes to nest building. Mr Lister went this week to prepare a nest box for one of his broody hens and found it full to the brim with every sort of bit and piece including the tail of a squirrel and in the middle of it was a tit sitting on her eggs. The box is, I suppose, at least a foot square and every bit had to be brought in through a small ventilation hole at the top of the box. It must have taken an immense amount of time and energy to build and it was rather bad luck on the occupier that it should be discovered at the end of it all. However, if she but knew she is a good deal safer in Mr Lister's hands than she might be otherwise.

A sharp frost such as we had last night is always unfair at this time of year. Last year, when we had ten degrees of frost on the 14th May, we thought that at last we had learned our lesson so we decided not to plant out anything ever again until after the middle of May. The population explosion of seedlings, however, forced our hands and yesterday, the 19th, we had to plant out some to make more room. Happily they seem to have survived the night, though the potatoes of neighbours have been burnt. One enthusiastic potato grower got up early and watered them before the sun got on to them which he said is the most effective way of stopping damage by frost bite. Our only casualty looks like being a Gunnera or Prickly Rhubarb whose leaves have ominous patches of brown. I have chucked some water over them in the hope that my neighbour is right but it seems a drastic cure. I can think of few things more likely to lower morale than after a frosty night in the open to be given a cold shower just when the sun is coming out and you think that at last you may get warm.

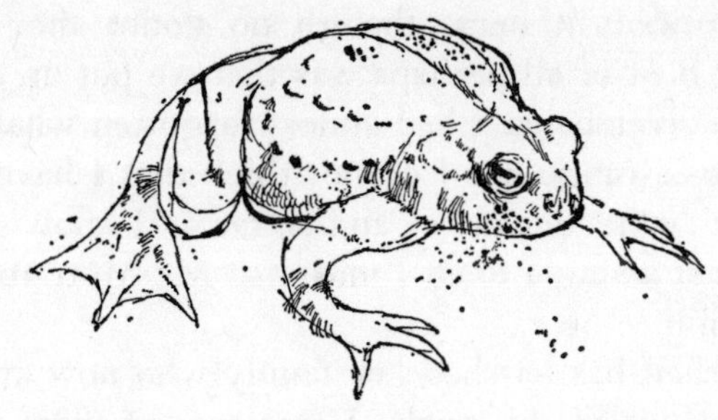

A Change of Valley

1st June

What luck it is that a warm sunny spell should come just at this time of year when everything is so fresh. Even in dull weather the countryside at this time always looks magnificent but when the sun shines, the birds sing, the bees buzz round the flowers and the shadows of the chestnut trees make dark round patches on the bright fresh green of the meadows, it looks superb. How sensible are the butterflies, few of whom, I read in that beautiful new book *Complete Butterflies in Colour* by L. H. Newman, will fly or feed, much less mate or lay their eggs, unless it is sunny.

We went over to cousins in the Itchen valley last week and had to admit that their valley is as good as ours. We arrived conditioned to be generous about it, as the long lane leading to their house was bordered by broad bands of Queen Anne's Lace through which clouds of buttercups poked their yellow heads. It is such a pity that hedge-cutting machinery has persuaded District Councils to cut it all down so ruthlessly in so many places. One would gladly pay a little extra on the rates to have it left wild rather than have to pay to have all the verges and hedges so severely trimmed.

It was interesting to see how much difference there is between two chalk stream valleys not very far apart. We noticed two small flowers quite common in their water meadows which I

35

have not noticed in ours, though no doubt they are there somewhere. Best of all perhaps was that we put up one or two frogs by the river bank. I had almost forgotten what they look like. It seems strange but I do not think that I have ever seen a frog in our water meadows and so far as I know our garden does not boast a single toad. I must ask Mr Mott about it next time I see him.

The moorhen has hatched her family who now swim fussily about in and out of the reeds. I saw two of them leave their nest for, I suspect, the first time as it was less than twenty-four hours after they had hatched out. They flopped off the edge of the nest on the side where the stream flows fastest and for the first second or two wobbled about so much that I thought they were going to capsize but as soon as they got into calm water they seemed completely at home as if they had been swimming about for weeks. The mother appears to take no notice of them but I see that she hustles them into hiding places when it looks as if anyone is coming too close.

As if the entertainment of watching all the busy scenes that go on all round us at this time of year is not enough, the young people in the village are giving us a performance of *Alice in Wonderland* in the Village Hall on Saturday evening to help our church. A great deal of hard work has been put into it and I am told that at rehearsals the enthusiastic vehemence with which the Queen of Hearts inveighs her favourite line 'Off with his head' often frightens the nervous.

A Port and Starboard Compromise

What a relief it is to those who live in the country when the weather plays fair at this time of year.

Not only does it mean so much to farmers and gardeners, but it is in these few summer months that people do what they can to help various good causes by opening their gardens to the public and by arranging fêtes and other outdoor festivities, and the result of all the hard work by those who help to run them can be so very seriously diminished by a wet afternoon.

Our village is no exception. Indeed for a very small community it must rank very high for the number of activities it supports.

Last Saturday there was a Grand Gala Performance of *Alice in Wonderland* in the Village Hall by the young people to help buy new hassocks for our Church. These were ordered immediately after the box-office takings were counted and finally checked and all are hoping that they will arrive in time for next Sunday. The Parish Church Council found it almost impossible to decide whether green or red ones would look better but an amicable compromise was arrived at whereby pews on the starboard side of the aisle will have green and those on the port side red.

The performance was a great success and much enjoyed on both sides of the curtain. None of the cast was sick in spite of several sepulchral prophetic pronouncements by some of the younger and less experienced actresses. The call boys somehow managed to track down all performers no matter where they had got to in time to take their cues, though there were, I am told, some anxious moments about which the audience were happily oblivious.

This Saturday in aid of the Mental Health Society over forty splendid prizes, generously contributed by members of the village and several worthy burghers of Stockbridge, were drawn for on the lawn of Test Lodge while teas were provided at a bob a nob by that well-known firm of caterers Mesdames Saunders and Lister, without whose voluntary help no village function of any importance would be complete, while Mr Burtenshaw, not content with fathering and so providing the White Rabbit, the Cook, and the Executioner for the Grand Gala Performance of the week before, spent a large part of the hot afternoon humping chairs and tables.

It was unfortunate that two of the best home-made prizes, a Dundee cake and a superb woolly rabbit, went to winners as far afield as London E.8 and Chudleigh in Devon, but the bottle of whisky was kept in the village and a bottle of sherry went back appropriately enough to the Peat Spade.

The following day the Leckford Estate opened the Longstock Water Garden to the public and £89 was raised to help towards paying for new lavatories for the Village Hall which means that the garden was seen by about a thousand visitors.

On Saturday the 29th June the Church Fête will be held in the Vicarage garden and already members of the village are getting busy about it. Last year the Fete raised £250, which went to maintain our Church and much was given away to various charities.

In these days of unrest, strikes, sit-ins, protests and riots one cannot help but think how pleasant it is to live among people who give up so much of their own time (when they might be dutifully striking, sitting in, protesting or rioting) to help not only their own immediate neighbours and community but also others less fortunate than themselves elsewhere. It is also pleasant to have lovely weather in which to do it.

Full Reward and a Glorious Fête

It is not often in this country that when you open the down-stairs windows first thing in the morning you are met by a waft of hot fresh air smelling of roses and peonies, but such was the case on the first day of July after ten days of almost continuous rain. The previous week had been an anxious one. The Church Fête was to be held on Saturday and spirits sank steadily lower as one of the great days of our year got closer and closer and still the rain persisted. I have no doubt that some of those backwoodsmen from Australia, who came over to follow the fortunes of their countrymen at Lord's and Wimbledon, expressed themselves well on the weather; but I suspect it was mere light-hearted banter compared with views expressed by members of the village, one or two of whom are naval pensioners and have therefore had a lifetime's practice at describing it.

For the first time our Fête was to be held on the last Saturday of June instead of the first Saturday in July. To the open maledictions of the weather were therefore added the muttered forebodings of some who said that to change the date was to interfere with nature, and that after the deluge would follow fire, pestilence and famine and that the Committee would be lucky if their action did not bring to the village all three at once.

All Friday it rained hard. Preparations were made to hold the Fête in the Village Hall instead of the Vicarage garden. The gentleman who had bought the old Methodist Hall was tracked down in Andover and generously and gladly gave his permission to use the hall as an overflow, provided somebody knew where the key was. Mr David Owen mustered his crew of helpers who loaded up the tractor-drawn trailers with benches

and tables and chairs and kept them in a barn overnight ready
to move at a moment's notice either to the Vicarage or to the
Village Hall, while stall-holders sought out macintoshes and
other waterproof coverings for their wares. In short, masterly
organisation dominated the scene.

Saturday morning broke dull and rainy. The fatal decision
was to be made at nine o'clock. About eight o'clock weather
information centres in the South of England were alerted by
telephone and soon were busy relaying information to Longstock. At nine o'clock the decision was made to hold the Fête
in the Vicarage garden. Immediately the village swung into
action. By noon the stalls and games and tables were all in
place. By 1.30 the sun was shining. By 2.30 brisk business was
being done and punctually at three o'clock the Fête was opened
by Mrs Loveless the wife of Dr Loveless, who like his father
and grandfather before him had looked after generations of
village families. It was immediately obvious that no more
popular choice of an opener could have been made. Home-made
bouquets were presented, one to Mrs Loveless by Jeanette Jones
and the other to the Chairwoman of the Committee by Glynis
Hunt, one of the leaders of the young people in the village. By
4.30 it was all over, with takings beating the previous record
by a few pounds.

On the following Sunday evening the Church was fuller than
it had been since Easter Day. There, no doubt, many gave
thanks for so wonderful and unexpected a sunny afternoon,
kneeling humbly (and more comfortably than for years) on the
new red and green hassocks that the young people had provided
from their box-office takings for their performance of *Alice in
Wonderland* a fortnight before.

Bird Song and Burgeoning

16th July

For weeks past there has been a bird who sings almost all daylight hours in one of our nearest big trees. He starts at dawn and then knocks off for an hour or so, presumably for breakfast, and starts again about half past seven.

I am no good at bird songs. Pheasants, cuckoos and ducks are about all on which I feel I can safely go *banco* and only very few of the smaller birds do I recognise. Even thrushes and blackbirds I am not certain about when heard separately. This particular little chap, however, was so persistent and his song dinned into me so often that I felt sure that I could remember it and was determined to find out what he was.

Many times I searched the tree but could never spot him among the very thick leaves of the sycamore in which he lives. Then one day last week I heard him very near and looked up and saw him sitting in the evening sun on the telephone wire immediately over my head. For a second or two I did not recognise him, he seemed to be all pink and soft dove grey and then he turned to preen himself and I saw that he was a cock chaffinch.

He obligingly stayed there singing away while I slipped indoors to get my field glasses to look at him more closely and was delighted that I did so. Unless you study birds you don't often notice them when they are almost above you when they look quite different and, in this particular case, prettier than ever. I felt a little ashamed at not recognising his song but felt better when I played a bird song record of a chaffinch and found that the recorded version was only slightly similar to this one's song, so I imagine that the songs of the same kind of bird can vary quite widely, which of course makes them all the more difficult to remember.

Whereas the songs of birds are growing less the countryside has reached its prime. The valley lies 'framed in the prodigality of nature'. The heavy rains that we have been having have helped the rich lushness of full summer to reach its peak.

They have also made the weeds grow until one despairs of keeping pace with them. Barrow load after barrow load is carted away until the compost heap can hold no more and a new one has to be started elsewhere and yet they still come. In fact one's whole time seems to be spent dizzily staking up flowers drooping under the weight of abundance or pulling up long lank weeds. So great is the pressure at times that it would not be surprising to find an occasional delphinium on the compost heap and some nettles carefully staked.

Moles have returned with a vengeance and tunnelled all through a new grass path which we sowed in the spring. Trapping has dealt with only one so I thought I would try putting down worm killer and compel the moles to search elsewhere only to find on reading the instructions that the potion should not be used on newly-sown grass. You can't win.

The Climax of the Year

When one comes to think of it this is quite a dramatic time of year. The corn begins to ripen in the fields, the water meadows turn a greyish green, the countryside's grown up and Nature nears the climax of the year – the harvest. The birds have grown silent and have finished bringing up their young, as also have other small fry, and now all wait for the great fruits of the earth on which all life depends and up to which everything has been leading for so many months.

Yesterday we took a day off and sat in the garden and looked at it all and thoroughly enjoyed what we saw. An occasional idle does us all good. As I sat there doing nothing I was reminded of an extract from the diary which my wife kept when we went by sea to Panama which read: 'Another lovely, hot, uneventful day. A piece of sea-weed went by at 2.40 p.m.'

The wrens I used to see in the winter have evidently raised a family. I found one very small one in our greenhouse this week. There was a full-grown hedge sparrow in it as well and both panicked when I arrived and fluttered desperately as they tried to find a way through the glass. I stood quite still and watched. After about a minute the tiny wren gave up trying and sat on a frame and just bleeped away in the depths of despair while the hedge sparrow still went on fluttering. This went on for about another half-minute until the continuous bleeping of the baby wren got on the house sparrow's nerves and then every few seconds she stopped her fluttering and went over to the wren and thrust her beak down the little one's throat as if feeding her and then rushed back to try and find a way out again. One could almost hear her say: 'Oh for goodness sake stop that ghastly bawling. I'm doing my best.'

Twice more that day I found the little wren back in the greenhouse and both times I remained quite still and let her calm down. I met her several times outside when she seemed to have got used to me for although she flew away she went off quite gently with no sign of panic.

I was therefore distressed next morning to find what I thought were her squashed remains on the road outside, run over by some passing car, but I think it must have been one of her brothers or sisters as I have seen two about quite often since, one of whom I am pretty sure is her.

Wrens have been very scarce round here since that bad winter four years ago so it is pleasant to see them coming back.

I found a young thrush lying dead in the road this morning in exactly the same place as I found the fledgeling wren. Cars must take a terrible toll of young birds at this time of year.

Through the Fog

12th August

Yesterday evening it stopped raining when the wind backed gently round to the South and the cloud cleared in time for us to watch a melancholy sun sink beyond the hill behind us. Melancholy or not it was a relief to see him and know that he was still about for we had not seen him for many days. A little later a dark yellow moon rose behind the black trees opposite to take the sun's place, but before she had time to glide very far along her path she was blotted out by a mist that filled the valley. I happened to wake up at about two o'clock in the morning and found our little world very damp and silent and very very dark. So, as the moon was nearly full, the fog must have been very thick. As I lay in bed I heard distinctly a reed foghorn. I thought at first that it could not be possible and that it must have been the hooter of some passing car some miles away on the A30; but the familiar grunt as it finished its note put any doubts to an end.

I listened for it to repeat itself but heard no more. I am certain that I did not dream it and that it was one of those queer tricks that fog plays at sea, and it must have come from forty miles away if it were, as I think, the Calshot Buoy.

It certainly brought back memories of many anxious moments at sea before the days of radar, when one drifted with little wind not knowing quite where one was, not daring to anchor lest one should be in a shipping lane and listening and listening to some distant fog signal or siren that seemed to come from a different point of the compass each time it sounded.

It reminded me too of one occasion when during fog I suddenly saw loom up not far away a huge shape that looked like some monstrous animal with a big fin on its back and a large fluked tail. I could not imagine what it could be and, being alone and a bit wrought up as one always is in fog, felt frightened in spite of telling myself that the days were long past when charts were marked with the warning that 'Here be monsters'.

As I peered through the fog the great tail moved and changed shape and for a moment I had to fight not to panic. Then I heard a bell ring and realised that it was a ship at anchor with the coiling wreaths of fog twisting her into strange shapes. It is no wonder that in the old days sailors returned full of superstitions and strange tales.

I once saw the sea light up all round us with lights flashing at regular intervals. Our position was miles away from any light and it became a sort of navigator's nightmare. I remember taking a bearing from an extra bright light flashing four every twenty seconds which I fixed as the Outer Gabbard nearly thirty miles away and a long way below the horizon. The phenomenon lasted quite a long time until the lights snapped out together as if controlled by a master switch. I am told that it is caused by some form of mirage and, though rare, such an experience is not by any means unknown in home waters.

I write this by the river and at my feet on the bank there is a big patch of water forget-me-nots, willow herb, water cress and water speedwell all in full flower and mixed up together. A far cry from strange phenomena at sea but equally impressive.

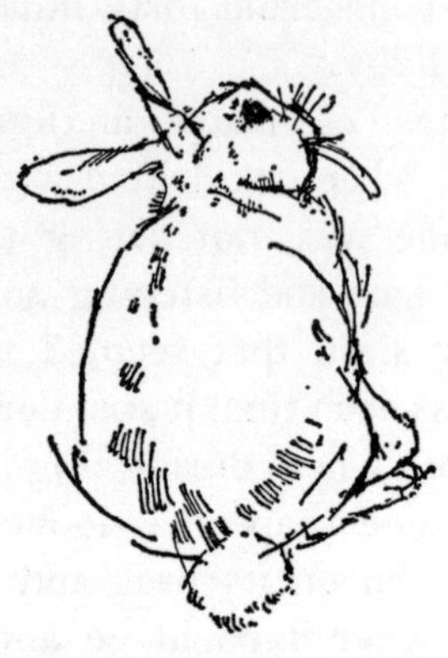

Return of the Rabbits

24th August

It looks very much as if the house martins have left and yet it is hard to believe that they should go so early. It seems only so very few weeks ago that we were watching them arrive. It may be that they have only gone temporarily elsewhere, but it is certain that two days ago there were hundreds of them swooping and diving about our lawn and sitting in twittering groups on the telephone wires and now there is not one to be seen.

We noticed them particularly as there were so many of them and we were wondering whether the smaller birds among them were their own young or some other kind of bird altogether. Suddenly they flew off at once with a whoosh that could be heard thirty yards away and my wife remarked on it, wondering what could possibly have frightened them all at once. It may be that it was not fright at all but that someone had twittered the equivalent of 'O.K. boys, let's go' and we had watched the start of their great trek of thousands of miles across seas, deserts and jungles to Southern Africa. If so, it was a good bit of luck or forethought on their part as the wind had just gone round to the north so they had it behind them on their way south.

We have been away for a fortnight and returned to find the garden in much better shape than it usually is after we have been away, thanks to two friends to whom we had lent the house and who had insisted on paying an outrageous rent by dead-heading and weeding the garden. My gratitude and admiration, however, suffered a sharp and sudden decline when they told me that, when they were resting and having a cup of tea in the summer house, they were fascinated by watching the young rabbits playing about by one of the flower beds by the river. I had suspected before we left that there was *a* rabbit lurking about, ever since I had found a precious Malva Mosachta almost nibbled to the ground; so any reader who has experienced having his Malva Mosachta nibbled by a rabbit will understand what my feelings were on being told that young rabbits were fascinating to watch.

It seems that rabbits are coming back very quickly as Mr Burtenshaw has told me that there are quite a number now in the gardens at Longstock Park where they are beginning to be a serious nuisance.

Many years ago the field next to our garden had a large rabbit warren, so it looks as if we are in for trouble, particularly as I notice that nearly all the Marigolds in the nearest flower bed to it have been eaten; though curiously enough the Carnations, usually thought by rabbits to be a pretty delectable dish, have hardly been touched. Maybe, as the rabbits are still very young, they have yet to find that out for themselves.

Infuriating though they are, I think that I would rather try and deal with rabbits than with moles, and anyway it makes a change.

The Start of Autumn

For the last three or four months many of us, I suspect, have been thinking to ourselves how nice it will be when summer really comes, but it was only this week that I gave up trying to fool myself any longer and faced the fact that this year it never will.

Seasons merge so gently into each other that it ought to be impossible to make up one's mind when one ends and the next begins, and yet there nearly always comes a moment, generally quite unexpected, when one says to oneself: 'This is it. The new season has begun.'

For a week or so the trees have been hanging out, here and there, a few yellow leaves of warning, but even the faint smell of a distant bonfire failed to shake my belief that summer still might come. It was not until this week, when I met two very small people walking down the lane carrying a basket, that I finally admitted that I could ignore the signs no longer. 'We have been blackberrying,' they said.

However foolish the practical people who consult calendars may have thought my idea that there still might be a whisper of a summer to come, I find myself in the genial company of one of our moorhens who I see has just hatched a chick; but I fear that it is no use pretending that one moorhen chick makes a summer any more than one swallow.

For the impractical who garden, this is an extremely difficult time of year. There is no room for anything. Nearly all plants have grown to an enormous size and one does not wish to cut them down because they are still more or less in flower, and yet there are masses of biennials, sown during flashes of forethought, gasping for lack of breathing space and which have to be planted out for next year in the hope that there may be a summer. Fortunately we go in for Sunflowers. These magnificent and sensible flowers have a convenient habit of not growing many leaves at the bottom of their stalks, so that there is generally room to squash in a few small plants round them. The difficulty is to remember that they are there when one comes to clean up; but in practice we find that a good many survive.

This method adds too to the pleasant surprise of finding in unexpected places small plants that one has forgotten about. I know perfectly well that they will still come as a mild shock in spite of having undergone very recently a three-day course in anti-surprise during a very welcome visit from grandchildren. After twenty-four hours one took almost as a matter of routine finding a large faded sunflower on one's desk, kindly and thoughtfully put there in case one wanted to preserve the seed, and a bunch of over-ripe poppy heads placed on a bed for presumably a similar reason. I admit that casually opening a box of matches and finding it filled with bits of cabbage leaves and a bright green caterpillar momentarily unnerved me, but this was largely due to a feeling of guilt because only that morning, when the caterpillar lived in a jam jar, I had been asked to be very careful not to frighten it.

Defeat of the Rabbits

21st September

People who live in the valley of a chalk stream are especially lucky in times of extreme wet such as we have been having recently. During the heavy rains which brought so much misery and disaster to other valleys in the South and East we have had little flooding. The river rose quickly but the water soon seeped away through the chalk and its level now seems little higher than in an ordinary winter.

Colour is fading fast from the water meadows but there are still bits of purple Loosestrife here and there and clumps of Hemp Agrimony left to brighten the banks, helped by some kind of Balsam with its curious little orange and yellow flowers that look like tiny plumed helmets with matching breast plates. These seem to be on the increase. I was told that they are fairly new arrivals here, having spread from the river Kennet near Newbury where they escaped from a private garden not so many years ago.

Colour is also beginning to disappear from the garden, though patches of Michaelmas Daisies, Dahlias and Chrysanthemums come to the rescue. Every year we think we ought to have more but are stopped from doing anything about it because it means sacrificing other plants to make room for them.

Another delightful patch of colour presently giving us great pleasure is a small scattering of hardy Cyclamen (Neapolitanum) among which this year we planted some Autumn Crocuses. The rabbits nearly spoilt it by making scrapes all over the patch and digging up the bulbs (or are they corms? I always forget the difference), but I defeated them just in time by rigging up round the patch a fence of garden string soaked in Reynardine two or three inches off the ground. It seems to have scared off the rabbits and the mauve of the Crocuses and the pink of the Cyclamen blend so well together that it is well worth the tumble or two that one takes when one forgets and trips up over the string, and getting the Reynardine on one's clothes so that one returns to the house smelling like a badger in desperate need of a bath.

This week we pulled up our Sweet Peas. A sad moment as they have given us so much enjoyment this summer. My wife had tended them daily for three months or more so she knew each plant's peculiar little ways and they were more like pets. On the other side of the coin, however, all indoor Chrysanthemums have been brought safely under cover and many are in bud, so they and the Perpetual Flowering Carnations should brighten up the dull days ahead, that is if the Carnations are going to do what I hope. I recently had some difficulty with them and wrote to a professional expert for advice, explaining what I had done and asking if there was anything else that I should do. I received a long and most helpful letter back, but he wound up by saying that in view of what I had told him he had no doubt that I would have no difficulty in rotting my cuttings. I am fairly certain that it was a misprint for 'rooting', but not confident enough to write and ask him. One would feel such a Charlie if it were not.

One Man Tried to Mow

5th October

We have had two days of warm sunny weather and the glass is still rising. St Luke's summer seems to have arrived. A little early perhaps, but none the less welcome for all that after such a long, long spell of dull drizzly days which made the grass grow too long and kept it too wet to cut. This meant that it was touch and go whether the lawn would have to be left until long enough to scythe, as a neighbour has had to do.

The few days on which it would have been possible to mow always seemed to be those on which there were more important things to do. One precious day in particular was lost in my case because of an optimistic and foolish decision to readjust the machine so that it would cut on the left side as well as on the right.

Admittedly I am a poor mechanic, but it took me all the afternoon to undo the various inaccessible nuts and bolts which the instruction book glibly said were to be loosened. Most of the nuts were seized up solid. The instruction book became more and more illegible as black grease spattered its pages. Few spanners seemed to fit, and those that did were impossible to turn more than an eighth of an inch before the handle hit some protuberance which was either too strong or looked too important to hammer out of the way.

At long last, however, the job was done. The blades of the roller were so microscopically adjusted that strips of paper were cut as cleanly as the most pernickety writer of an instruction book could desire, no matter whether I inserted them right side, left side or even in the middle. I bolted the whole beastly contraption together again and, setting the gear at full speed to make up for lost time, started to mow.

The clatter it made – similar, I imagine, to the noise of the battle of Alamein at the time of crisis when both sides flung in every tank they had got – told me only too clearly that something was still not right. Fortunately it was then too late to go through the whole performance again so I thankfully turned aside from the higher flights of complicated mechanical engineering and turned with relief to a simple spade and started the autumn digging.

When you have reached the age when you no longer want to take strenuous exercise, either for fun or to keep your weight down, there are worse ways of spending a calm still October afternoon than digging quietly away while a robin watches and

rooks caw in the trees a field or two away. Your mind free-
wheels gently round days long gone by and dips occasionally
into wildly impracticable plans for the future until the time
comes when there is a slight nip in the air as the mist creeps
across the valley, the light begins to fade and you are called in for
a late tea with hot buttered toast and, after a few mouthfuls,
put back all the ounces you have just so pleasantly shed.

But why worry? You can knock them off again tomorrow if
the digging weather holds; and if it doesn't, well what's an
ounce or two compared with peace of mind? And even if some
pang of puritanical conscience forbids you to have too much
peace of mind there is always the blasted mower to adjust.

Admirable Admirals

19th October

A neighbour who lives on the other side of the valley told
me that on one of the recent sunny days he had counted no less
than forty Red Admiral butterflies in his garden on one small
patch of Michaelmas Daisies, and said that there were about
another forty or so of other kinds. He added that he had seldom
if ever seen so large a collection in so small an area before. This,
coming from someone like him, is quite something because,
not only is he one of the world's leading authorities on spiders,
but he knows a great deal about other small creatures too,
unlike so many of us who take only an idle interest in hearing
about small happenings such as a large cluster of butterflies on
a bush at this time of year.

He told me that Red Admirals are migratory, so when I got

home I looked them up in a book because it seemed extraordinary to me that so small and ungainly a thing as a butterfly should have the stamina to be able to fly great distances.

I was astonished to read that they come from as far away as the Mediterranean area and that, although some stay through the winter and survive, many go back again at the end of the season. It seems unbelievable that they can fly so far. Yet I suppose, when one comes to think of it, that they must have been given such big wings for some very good reason. Nature is, after all, remarkably practical and those of her children who fail to be so soon pay the ultimate penalty and cease to exist.

I was interested to read also that the name Admiral is comparatively modern. In the eighteenth century they were known as Admirable butterflies, a much more sensible name as who cannot help admiring such a beautiful combination of shape, colour and design.

I learnt too that some caterpillars, not those of the Red Admirals apparently, smell like goats. I can't say that I have ever thought of smelling a caterpillar, but have now definitely decided never to try.

Not a Good Year for Saints

3rd November

Because we had had two days of sunny weather I wrote a month ago that it seemed that St Luke's summer had arrived. I blush when I think of it because it has rained almost continuously from that moment and it was not until yesterday that we saw

the sun again when a strong cold north wind cleared the clouds
away and began stripping the trees in earnest.

A strong north wind at this time of year is particularly
welcome, so far as we are concerned, as it blows the leaves
from our trees into a field instead of on to our lawn. It is the
first time that this has happened for a long time as usually at
this time of year there are a good number of southerly gales
that get in first. Luck was on our side in other ways too. In
fact it has been a remarkably propitious start to the leaf-
sweeping season.

Grandchildren, for instance, arrived in numbers and wanted
a bonfire to celebrate Guy Fawkes' day and were soon led to
believe by smooth sales talk and a pint of paraffin that leaves
are highly combustible. Gordon, Tony and Paul, three small
boys who live down the road, also turned up to demand their
Danegeld in the form of asking for a job and were immediately
put to work with brooms and rakes with which they attacked
the lawn and, after ten minutes or so, each other, with con-
siderable vigour. It is true that they thrust a large proportion
of the leaves down each other's necks, but, although in con-
sequence the leaves never reached the bonfire, they no longer
littered the lawn. It takes, however, a very large shirt indeed
to make filling it with leaves a viable commercial proposition

even at a shilling, but labour relations, always a bit delicate where those three are concerned, were reasonably stable at the time so I thought it wiser not to insist on my contractual right and have the leaves transferred from shirts to bonfire.

The bright sun yesterday gave us all a chance to enjoy the autumn colours to the full almost for the first time this year. There are many yew trees round about and some of the roads are lined with them. They make a splendid contrast to the light copper and yellow of the other trees in the hedges and are often a beautiful sight in themselves. This is especially true when the Traveller's Joy has scrambled up inside them and spilled out over the tops and sides making them look in the sun as if someone has taken swipes at them with a giant whitewash brush.

This morning, for the first time this autumn, the puddles on the sides of the lanes have a thin skin of ice glinting in the bright sun, which reminds one to get busy about covering up delicate plants and shrubs and also, alas, that St Luke has rather let the side down with his summer, and also St Martin with his. But as St Martin is a lesser saint and also, poor chap, has to do his stuff in November, we don't expect so much from him.

Seals, Kipling and Rascals

18th November

I have just been reading a small booklet called *Our Village* written by Miss Winifred Beddington who until quite recently lived in Longstock. In it she set down information about the village, which, although still well known to most of those who live here, will soon be swamped and forgotten as the older generations move on and newcomers arrive to take their place.

Most of us are told or hear about small matters trivial and unimportant in themselves but which occasionally connect up with something that someone else has been told and so could easily grow into a story. Some day perhaps little bits of information like those written down by Miss Beddington will be computerised with similar notes by others and out of it will come a detailed history of English village life which will make fascinating reading in years to come. Up to now so many stories and songs of times gone by are almost certainly based on facts of which there are no records.

Many years ago, thirty-nine to be precise, as I see that I made a note of the date at the time, I had a good example of this.

I was living alone miles away on the banks of a river in North Bengal. Every two months or so an old retired Hooghli pilot, a Captain Kearns, used to make a journey up the river on some inspection or other and used to stop and stay the night at my bungalow where, needless to say, he was always extremely welcome as I was living alone and had no neighbours.

He was a fine looking old boy and a delightful character and over a bottle of whisky we used to sit long into the night while I listened to his stories of the past. As the whisky in the bottle sank lower and lower, so his stories got taller and taller until sometimes they were hard to believe, and yet I am sure that even the most outrageous were founded on some vestige of fact.

I remember that he once told me a thrilling story about how some poaching sealing vessel bluffed some other out of the sealing grounds by pretending to be a Russian gunboat, and when the bluff was discovered how the crews fought it out to the death in the ice and fog in the desolate Bering Sea. His story had a familiar ring about it, so I went and got my Kipling and read him The Rhyme of the Three Sealers, to which he listened with wrapt attention never having heard it before. He told me that it was quite true and gave me the names of two of the skippers and I wrote them down there and then in my copy.

One was Maclaren and the other was Johnny Kiernan; he could not remember the name of the third. He told me at the same time that Kipling was wrong in telling his readers that a Matka was a she-seal; it was a bull seal. He also told me that Kipling was not quite right about a 'Holloschickee' being a young seal. Captain Kearns said that strictly speaking it meant a seal up to six years old.

He had been a sealer himself at one time and told me that it was a good life and well paid, unlike that of a whaler which he said was terrible and that whaling ships were manned for the most part by 'rascals'.

In spite of the adventurous life that he had led, I never heard the old gentleman use bad language, the term 'rascal' was the nearest that he ever got to it and, although we were quite alone and no lady was within fifty miles of us at least, the word 'rascal' had to be whispered.

He had, of course, come across a number of rascals in his time but the one that evidently made the deepest impression, for he told me about him more than once, was the gentleman in San Francisco who sold him a dead man for a dollar when, as the mate of his ship, he was trying to collect a few hands to take the place of his crew who had deserted to join the gold rush. Captain Kearns always used to shake his head sadly as he finished this yarn and there was a pause while he brooded over the rascality of the man, but also, it always seemed to me, over the loss of the dollar which he told me the captain of his ship refused to pay out of the ship's fund and made him pay it himself.

Many were the stories he told me during those evenings. So often I wish that I had followed the excellent example of someone like Miss Beddington and had written them down before they were forgotten.

Guinea-Gold and Coral-Copper

During a motor drive last week on one of the few cloudless days we have had for some time my wife and I found ourselves telling each other that we had never seen the autumn colours so beautiful but then remembered that on several occasions we had said that in other years.

On a fine day all trees and hedges look superb in their autumn colours against the background of a pale autumn sky, but what made it exceptional this year were the elms.

Presumably because of the wet and the absence of frost the elms and the ash were green until well into November and I noticed that in the case of the ash particularly they started shedding their leaves while still green; something that I had not seen during the seven autumns that we have been here and which was confirmed by Mr Bookham who told me that he had not seen it happen before in the sixty odd years that he had lived here.

Then came a mild frost and in two days the whole countryside was transformed. Every elm in the district became as yellow as a guinea and other trees turned colour as well, but it was the deep rich butter yellow of the great elms that stole the autumn show.

It only lasted for a very short time – two or three days at the most before they started shedding their leaves. Then for some days they had that tattered straggly look before they stood black and bare waiting for winter. Our little Liquidamber, however, seems reluctant to be deciduous and its pink and coral-copper leaves still make a pretty patch of colour against the background of reeds and river just as we had hoped.

The boring chore of leaf-sweeping is nearly over and one now has the satisfaction as one sweeps that it must be for the last time this season. Dull job as it is it has its dramatic moments. Yesterday afternoon, after three dreary hours of sweeping, I suddenly found myself uncovering two large molehills like dromedary's humps in an area in which up to that moment I thought no mole had ventured. So, like the psalmist of long ago, 'My heart was hot within me, while I was musing the fire burned and I spake with my tongue'. Not that any mole hereabouts would give a continental damn however much I spake but I felt the better for it and it added so much energy to my sweeping that I nearly broke the broom.

The birds seem to be singing much more than they usually do at this time of year. Mr Monger, who lives very close to the woods in the water garden, told me some days ago that as day dawns each morning he hears a thrush singing just outside his front door. It so happened that I called to see Mr Monger on the morning of the 2nd December at 11.30 o'clock and the thrush he spoke about was still going great guns in the tree above us as we talked, and a lovely sound it was too.

Because of this I listened particularly carefully at the end of the day and found that there was quite a concert going on all round, though nothing, of course, like those in May. But then so many members of the choir are away just now enjoying themselves abroad.

Signs and Portents

15th December

Much as the seers of ancient times studied the flights of birds that foretold happenings of great import, so we at this end of Longstock study Mr Fudge's garden in which there is a tree which, when lit up, tells us and all those who pass by that Christmas time has once more come round.

Although most of us admit that the news of enormous crowds of shoppers in Oxford Street, pictures of the lights in Regent Street and reports that the Norwegian Ambassador has switched on the lights of the huge Christmas tree in Trafalgar Square are strong evidence that Christmas is coming, some of the older and more cautious of us would feel just a bit more confident if, failing Mr Fudge's tree being actually lit up, there were even small portents such as a bit of electric cable dangling from one of his windows or a ladder lying about on the lawn near the tree; but up to now there is no sign.

The young, however, with that carefree optimism of youth are prepared to chance it and are already busy about a Nativity Play to be performed in the Village Hall on Sunday the 22nd December at 3 p.m.

I learnt this from my friend 'Peanuts' who came round one day this week to negotiate a contract for helping me sweep the last remaining leaves that here and there still litter the lawn. His proposed terms seemed reasonable enough at the time but in practice I found that, when calculated on the basis of 'per leaf swept' they were exorbitant, especially as I had overlooked 'Peanuts' ' occupancy cost of valuable space in the wheelbarrow itself.

During a comparatively quiet spell on the way to the compost heap, when he explained that he was preventing the leaves from falling out of the barrow by sitting on them, he told me that there was also to be a play at his school. I asked him if he himself were going to perform, but he said that there was no part for him and anyway he was no good at acting. I would have thought myself, however, that he could easily have been worked in somehow, say a very brief walking-on part right at the beginning which would make it obvious to the audience why the shepherds thought it advisable to watch their flocks – a part that I'm pretty certain would be within his histrionic capacity. It is possible, of course, that the producer did have some such idea but did not care to risk it.

It seems a good year for holly and many of the trees round about have plenty of berries, though the birds are making big inroads on them. Our own little tree, planted two years ago, had berries for the first time, but when I went to protect them with a net I found that I was too late.

It is going to be touch and go whether our Chrysanthemums will last long enough to make up for the absence of our own holly, but the winter Jasmine is out, so, with a fair picking of our faithful Perpetual Flowering Carnations, we should be able to decorate our house in celebration of the Great Day as soon as Mr Fudge's tree sends out its friendly message of rejoicing and goodwill, telling us all that it is time to join in.

Christmas as Usual

28th December

In spite of the great interest that the whole world took in the tremendous voyage by three men to the moon and back, it is clear that it will take a good deal more than that to disturb the quiet unruffled dignity with which Longstock celebrates and enjoys Christmas. It was as if the Christmas cards, the lessons in church and the Nativity Play in the Village Hall had all helped to remind us unconsciously that three kingly men had once before made a journey that was to mark an event of tremendous importance to the world and that this recent journey to the moon, wonderful as it might be, was not going to be allowed to change our ways or shake our beliefs.

Our Nativity Play produced by Glynis Hunt was well done by the young people of the village who played to a large audience made up of all and sundry whose ages ranged from Miss Ledbrooke's ten months to Mrs Goater's ninety years and

which included the village hall robin, age unknown, who flew in as the play was beginning to watch as well.

The Old People's Club held its Christmas tea which the robin also attended, though it is doubtful if he is entitled to be a fully paid up member, and, if a few members had resigned since last year to join some equally happy celestial club elsewhere, others in the village had grown up enough to qualify for membership and take their places.

Once again Mr Tewkesbury brought over a small team from the Winchester Cathedral choir to sing at our carol service and backed it up not only with members of the choir of St Nicholas of Leckford but also with a past member of the choir of King's College, Cambridge, so it was quite a memorable musical service. Perhaps too it may become memorable because one of the passages from the Bible which were read between the carols was beautifully read in a homely Hampshire accent by Mr Somerton, a staunch Methodist and a fine Christian, as well as being a master thatcher, who did his share, as much as any Moderator or Bishop, to help unite again members of the Protestant faith.

In writing about our Christmas one must not forget our Young Church Builders who visited various houses and once more collected a goodly sum largely for the church but from which, they told me, a small sum was to be held back to help buy a curry comb and brush as a Christmas present for one of the horses that they ride and who, they told me, wants them very much.

It will be seen, therefore, that Christmas has come and gone in much the same way as always and it is doubtful if it could be improved. The only difference from other years has been perhaps that the Snowdrops at the foot of the Ginko tree outside the church failed to bloom in time for Christmas Day, but it is doubtful if anybody noticed this except Mrs Mason who has known them since she was a child a good many years ago now. It is, after all, a very small clump.

1969

Confirmation of Spring

The grass on our lawn under the trees is prickling with shoots of Snowdrops. One or two of the earlier varieties are in flower and can be seen from the house bravely leading the way to the new year. Soon they will be in their full glory.

We are getting a bonus of extra pleasure from them this year because, when we put some more down in the autumn to join those already there, we were not quite sure if we had put them in the right place as we had to plant them from memory; but we find that we had got it just right so the new ones are already known as the Pelman plot.

Other newcomers are some winter Aconites beginning to turn yellow, so that, although there may well be grim days ahead, the coming of spring is once more confirmed and no amount of dull wet drizzly days can deny it.

Unpleasant though it will be, a return to hard winter conditions would be welcome as things seem to be pushing on a bit too fast and, if they continue at this rate, they will take a very severe knock later when there is a cold snap, and also many of the plants and bushes need a rest. It was a very late autumn and many trees carried their leaves well into November.

A number of the big bulbs are pushing their way through, but there are no signs yet of the Crocuses, though I search diligently for them. So diligently in fact that a passing motorist, seeing me walking slowly about stooping right down with my head barely eighteen inches from the ground, stopped and asked me if I were all right. This struck me as funny though friendly, so, grinning broadly, I said that I was, whereupon he made off very quickly, looking, I thought, a bit frightened.

We are particularly anxious about the Crocuses because last year we lost so many eaten by mice that we had to plant a lot more to take their place and this time planted each one with a flake of naphthalene alongside it, which we were told would keep mice away, and we are keen to know if this dodge has worked.

In spite of the dull cloudy weather we have been enjoying a series of most wonderful sunrises these last few days. At this time of year, when the sun rises behind the hill on the far side of the valley, it seems to be just at the right angle to reflect its light so that the river looks like a crimson ribbon running through the soft greys of the water meadows. It may be that this is no exception but is because one notices the sunrises more in these days of the new winter time; but whether this is so or not, the fact remains that they have been a splendid sight and well worth waiting and watching for.

The rabbits that have been so troublesome in our garden have got myxomatosis again, poor little devils. It is a dreadful disease to see and one can't help feeling terribly sorry for them in spite of the frightful damage that they do.

Spring Song and Quick Tempers

The weather, at the time of writing, continues very mild and wet. Everything is in bud, the Snowdrops almost at their best, and there is a sprinkling of yellow Crocuses here and there on our bank, with, one hopes, many more to come; and so we stand once more at the gateway of the year.

Nor are these the only signs. One lovely warm sunny day last week the thrush that has sung to us so regularly the last two or three years from a particular branch on a particular tree was singing away in the same place as if spring were already here, and how much more sensible it is to sit on a branch and sing about it than go about like the rest of us shaking our heads and muttering that we will pay for it all later on.

On the same day a friend told me that he was up on the downland on the other side of the valley and had seldom heard the larks sing so gaily. Of all bird songs I think that the lark's is the most beautiful, but this may be because I am prejudiced. I so well remember, though it is now many many years ago, listening to a lark soaring over the South Downs and singing fit to bust. It was a wonderful spring day, warm and sunny and smelling of gorse and hot downland grass. Sitting beside me as I listened was a pretty girl in a pale blue cotton frock holding in her hands a small bunch of wild flowers that she had just picked. I was very much in love. I suggest to all young ornithologists, or for that matter any young man, that there are no more pleasant circumstances in which to listen to a lark.

At the bottom of our garden by the river we have an awkward bit of land which we have won back from the reeds. It is difficult to keep tidy because, being very low lying, it is often too soft to mow and if it is left the reeds come back and smother the grass. We have found that for a cupful of barley a day the wild ducks keep the jungle back and save us the bother and work of keeping it down with scythe or sickle. It is, I fear a form of sweated labour because it must take a great deal of quacking and trampling and shovelling about with a beak before they find a grain or two, but they seem to find it worth their while. It is certainly a very cheap way of keeping that bit close cropped and at this time of year the drakes look very decorative, for which they make no extra charge. I notice that there is now some tetchiness among them and that there is a good deal of squabbling, not over the barley but over the ladies, and already some seem to be pairing up for keeps.

Quick tempers are not confined to the drakes. I saw a tremendous fight between two blackbirds on our lawn this week. It went on I should say for over a minute – an exceptionally long time for a scuffle of this sort – with neither

bird giving way. At one moment one of them was down on his back with the other bird hammering away at him until I thought that he would do him real damage, but at last one admitted defeat and half flew and half hopped to five yards away. The victor was, however, not content and made him go another five yards and then another, and it was not until there was an interval of twenty yards between them that he was satisfied and settled down to beetle hunting once more.

A Trumpet Voluntary

1st March

The ice cold winds and the snow have put an end to all thoughts of gardening, which is a bore in some ways but a relief to the strain on one's conscience when there are other more important and less pleasant things to be done.

It also gives one time to think ahead and so avoid some simple mistake or omission which may wreck a gardening plan for the whole season. In the excitement of anticipation it is so easy to overlook some apparently insignificant precaution to prevent something happening from which a major disaster may spring.

I remember a good example of this from many years ago when I was a trooper in a volunteer cavalry regiment.

We had in our troop a splendid chap called Jones – a fine upstanding Welshman with a magnificent cavalry moustache which was much admired by all the ladies. In fact there was no doubt at all that when Trooper Jones was booted and spurred and girt about with sword and helmet and chains he was the perfect example of Nature's protective colouring – he looked a warrior.

One day Trooper Jones was wandering through the Quarter-master's stores, for what nefarious purpose I forget, when his eye lit upon the regimental trumpet which had long fallen into disuse because no one knew how to blow it. The sight of it evidently stirred within him some dormant primeval instinct dating back to the mists of ages when some distant forebear, dressed in Druid's robes, sent blasts on a ram's horn echoing through the valleys summoning the tribes to some local Eisteddfod.

Like so many Welshmen, Jones was a natural musician and, picking up the trumpet, found no difficulty in making it work and immediately appointed himself regimental trumpeter. Thereafter at our weekly drills we pranced round the parade ground accompanied by Trumpeter Jones blowing at intervals a variety of encouraging calls, such as 'Lights out', 'Water your horses' and 'Orderly Corporals', interspersed with other stirring calls of his own composition, with every now and then a few bars of 'Land of our Fathers' thrown in for good measure, and we all felt very proud indeed.

And then one day our great opportunity came. It was decreed that, in order to celebrate some important public occasion, there should be a great ceremonial parade which would be attended by the local Maharajah and the General Officer commanding the forces in the district and an assembled mass of His Majesty's loyal subjects, and we, as cavalry of the line, were to lead the march-past at this grand spectacle of Britain's military might. We had many a rehearsal and we all knew what was expected of us and were determined to do justice to the occasion.

We were sitting round polishing our equipment the evening before the great day when someone suggested that what would put the finishing touch to the glorious scene would be that when Trumpeter Jones rode out in front of the regiment with the Commanding Officer leading the march-past, he should be mounted on a white horse. The idea immediately fired Jones' celtic imagination and he forthwith left us and opened up negotiations with one of the local livery stables for the hire of a white horse for the following day. These were eventually successfully concluded and we all gladly contributed our share.

The next day came well up to everybody's expectations; the sun shone, the bands played, the guns fired and there was a hum and buzz of excitement among the crowd as the various regiments performed their evolutions, and then at last came the great moment when our regiment wheeled and jingled into line for the march-past with the Colonel and Trumpeter Jones some twenty yards ahead. As we approached the saluting base we could all see, even from astern, Trumpeter Jones' manly bosom swell with pride and air pressure as he prepared to blow a blast, compared with which the Last Trump would seem the merest chirrup on a penny whistle.

It was then that our failure to remember to take an apparently insignificant precaution found us out. Not one of us had remembered to tell the horse. No sooner had the first note started on its way than Trumpeter Jones was jet propelled in a perfect parabola, to the wonder of the assembled masses and the obvious irritation of the local General.

Looking back on it one cannot altogether blame the horse because, after all, a horse's ears are singularly ill placed when he's got a man on board who suddenly wants to blow a trumpet. Nor, indeed, can one really blame the General for making a scene and thereby adding to the confusion, for the sight of

Trumpeter Jones standing among the now disordered ranks, rubbing his behind with one hand and with the other raising to high heaven his trumpet, which now resembled a battered French horn, and calling on his pagan gods in his native Welsh to rain down thunderbolts on all white horses everywhere, but particularly on the one owned by the livery stable, must have detracted seriously from the military scene.

Poor Jones was inconsolable and felt the loss of his trumpet very keenly, so keenly in fact that we all felt that we should do something about it. It was accordingly proposed and unanimously carried that he should be appointed Farrier Sergeant, to which honorary rank he was elected with acclamation, and, while this did not make up altogether for the loss of his trumpet, it did mean that on ceremonial occasions in future he would go on parade carrying a battle axe, which we all told him was every bit as romantic and, as the sergeant major who was a regular told him, was in his hands at any rate a sanguinary sight less dangerous.

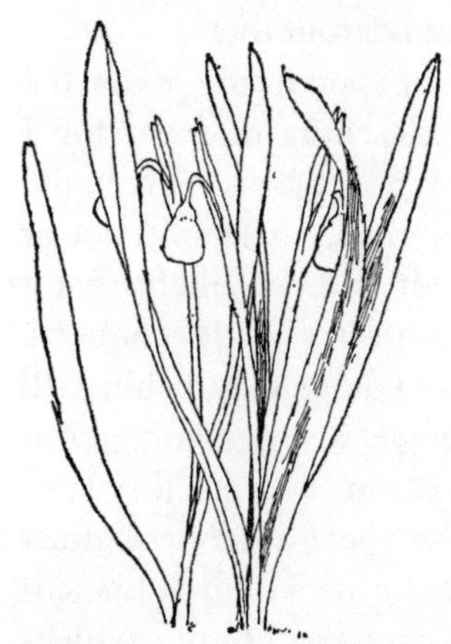

Glimmers of Spring

10th March

At long last some really heavenly days, or more accurately half days, for after bitterly cold nights we wake engulfed in thick fog. At first visibility is down to twenty yards or less, which slowly increases until about noon when the bright white disc of the sun shines faintly over the trees and starts sucking up the light grey mist until it warms the shivering world and one feels that this year's long harsh winter is beginning to loosen its hold. Certainly one or two birds round about feel it. Yesterday one, a chaffinch I think, spent much of the afternoon singing as if spring were already here and eventually persuaded one or two others to join in, if only half-heartedly; but he has given general encouragement because this morning, in spite of the fog, I heard a thrush sing his welcome to the dawn.

Another encouraging glimmer of spring days to come was seeing three robins at once about our bird table. We have always had one throughout the winter, and during the last week or two there have been occasionally two, but we have seldom if ever seen three together. While we watched, the newcomer started showing off to the other two from a few yards away, strutting about and stretching as high as he could with his head pushed right back and showing off his red waistcoat to its best advantage as if he had just paid a visit to Carnaby Street. The other two seemed to take no notice, but suddenly one of them fell for it and went over to the little dancer and in a second or two they flew off together.

The third remained sitting huddled up pondering over the fickleness of women or maybe the faithlessness of men, for I cannot tell the difference between a cock and a hen. Nor would I like to guess as I doubt if any but the most hardened man or woman hater would like to say whether it is more likely that a young gentleman robin will fall for a pretty little coquette pirouetting about in front of him, than a young lady robin will fall for a swashbuckling young gentleman swaggering about showing off his manly bosom encased in a smashing red waistcoat. I think, however, in this case the gooseberry must have been a hen as I don't think any young cock worth his salt would not have put up a fight in the circumstances; but whichever way it was the incident seemed soon forgotten and the aching heart found solace in an extra ration of Swoop on the bird table.

One compensation for the long drawn out tough winter is that it has preserved the early Snowdrops which are still in full bloom after six weeks of flowering. We have collected Snow-drops since we have been here. They have come from various sources, mostly given by kind friends who have a surplus, and others we have bought from time to time when we have found them going cheap and sometimes a dozen or so at full price when we have come across them in a shop and the mood has taken us. The result is that we have now several different kinds all mixed together, some early some late some large and some small, but of them all our favourites are the ordinary common variety which we planted when we first came here. These sturdy little flowers come out in January and have multiplied over the years to what is now quite a quantity. It is, however, the first time that we have seen them all out together. It is true that we have a few exotic giant ones not yet out, but these long lovely creatures do not risk their debut until April when all the little ones have taken their bow and in any case there are not enough of them to make much of a show, so they hardly count.

The Lingering Grip of Winter

25th March

Winter still holds us fast in its savage grip. All of us, plants, people, animals and birds are hard pressed to fight our way through to the spring, of which there is so little sign at present even though it has now officially begun and the days are at last longer than the nights.

Farmers are away behind schedule and gardeners still further, neither able to do very much until the ground gets warmer and dries out a bit. I see from my diary that we mowed our lawn last year for the first time on the 19th March, but this year, even if it were not to rain for several days, it would be impossible to do it for about a week even if it were necessary. Snowdrops are still in flower, though past their best, and Crocuses would make a gay sight if the sun were to shine. These of all flowers need to be seen in the sun to be appreciated in their full glory. A Primrose or two, short stalked and tiny, sit huddled among their leaves, and Daffodils have green buds ready to respond to any encouragement. One feels that a few days of warm sun would bring everything rushing out and we long desperately for it to happen; but, as soon as the sun breaks through, high thick cloud comes swooping up from the East and blots it out almost before we have time to recognise it.

However, in spite of all this, there is no doubt that spring will come after all. The garden is full of buds waiting to burst through, and Mrs Nation tells me that she has one precocious Daffodil in flower outside her little house. So things might be worse, if they could not be colder.

Another bright spot so far as we are concerned is that it looks as if the birds are leaving our Forsythias alone for the first time in seven years. One wonders why they should suddenly change their habits in this way. They must be very largely the same birds who have pecked at them so destructively over the last few years and they are most certainly the same Forsythias. A neighbour has told me that he has experienced the same thing with his Primulas; the birds this year suddenly seem to have got tired of them.

I have blamed sparrows and mice for going for our Crocuses and, though I cannot exonerate mice altogether – many of the Crocuses in a very mousey area have not come up at all in spite of the naphthalene I planted with the bulbs – I believe the damage done to the flowers is not by sparrows so much as by a thrush and one particular thrush at that. I have twice seen a thrush fly down low and pick a yellow Crocus off its stalk leaving it lying on the ground without stopping. I think the thrush must do it for amusement, a sort of bird tent pegging, and I don't blame him as it must be great fun to do.

As if we did not suffer enough from wild pigeons, we have made a dovecote, or rather a 'doocot', as my smart friends tell me I must say, and put it up in the garden. My gardening neighbours look at it a bit askance, even though as yet it is not occupied, but I don't think a 'doo' or two can add much to the general holocaust.

Spring Arrives

7th April

This must be one of the most backward springs for a long time, but it looks as if the sunny days at Easter have shaken us free at last from winter, which retreated still fighting, despite the sun, with its vicious cold East wind.

Even the ladies of the village were hard pressed to find enough flowers with which to decorate the church, but, with a few handfuls of Daffodils culled from Heaven knows where and a bunch or two of Forsythia and Iris Stylosa, they made up for lack of quantity by a delicate mixture of colouring. But today, Easter Monday, winter seems to have finally surrendered. The cold East wind has gone and we are left with a wonderful warm sun, with birds singing and Daffodils bursting out all round us. The trees still look bare, but the buds are there if one looks closely enough and one begins to wonder why we ever doubted that spring would come. On a day like this one feels that, if everyone had the chance of living in our valley for these next two months, no one, however well off, would want to strike because someone living in some other country earned a bit more, or that people would want to riot over religious beliefs or bash hell's bells out of somebody else because of political beliefs, or do any of the peculiar things that all people of all upbringings, culture and race apparently want to do these days and, one suspects, always have done.

It looks as if our new dovecote is soon going to add its quota to the general unrest. It has only been up about a week but already I have seen starlings go in and out of it, presumably house hunting. It will be interesting to see if they decide to squat. If they do I am not sure what will happen when the white fan-tailed pigeons arrive on the scene, but I suspect we will have a colour problem on our hands. Perhaps they may work out some sort of apartheid system of their own. There is plenty of room under the roof where pigeons cannot enter and which is the sort of place where starlings would naturally like to nest, so it may work out all right provided some fool of a pigeon does not refer to it as an attic instead of a penthouse.

Work in the gardens is now suddenly beginning in all seriousness. This morning a friend, who lives in one of the cottages up the road, while working in his garden saw me pass and remembered that he had promised me a root of a plant that I had much admired in his garden. He very kindly brought it round and we spent a delightful three-quarters of an hour discussing how this sudden change of weather made us all so busy and what a mad rush it all has become. During the course of this he told me that his wife always cuts his Forsythia hedge back hard so that it always has to flower on the old wood. According to my books this should be fatal, yet his hedge is always a splendid sight.

No news of the cuckoo yet. Last year the first time that anyone heard him here was the 5th April and today is the 7th. I hope he is not going to be too late; one always feels that the cuckoo's call slams the door on winter.

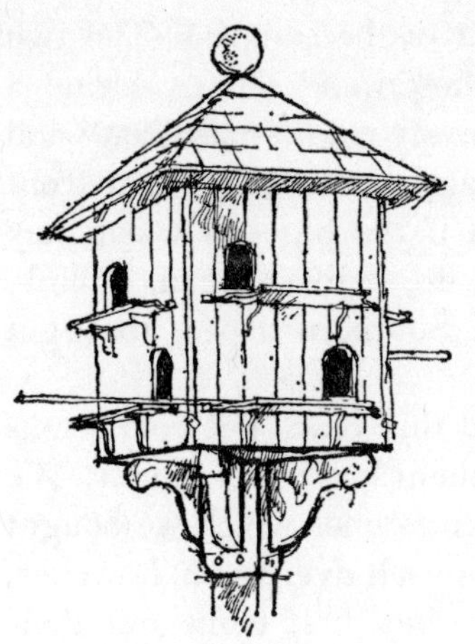

Summer Visitors Arrive

19th April

I am told that a cuckoo has arrived, in fact was heard by Mrs Debenham as long ago as Easter Sunday and seen, though not heard, by her husband two days later. Several others have heard him but I think that he must be the only one, or if there are others they are tactfully keeping their mouths shut while the cold, and today drizzly, weather lasts. However, the fact that he is here has given all of us the encouragement we need, for, although we have been having welcome sun, the cold (ten degrees of frost in the water garden two nights ago) has kept the trees still bare and the hedges, even now towards the end of April, are only just beginning to green up. Other summer visitors are beginning to turn up and I have just heard a grasshopper warbler announce his arrival at the bottom of our garden.

As we suspected, the starlings had moved into our dovecote and have had to be evicted. We found that it was not one pair but a whole colony. Not only had they taken over all the space under the roof, but had occupied two of the flats as well and were obviously going to take over the remainder as they were busy staking out their claims with bits of straw.

It seems that there must be a housing shortage in the starling world because the dovecote had only been up a very short time before it was seized upon. It is a square one divided into eight flats with two flats facing each point of the compass. The two facing North were the first to be chosen and chosen during a spell when there was a particularly nasty cold North-East wind blowing which must have blown straight in through their front doors. It will be interesting to see if the pigeons when they come make the same choice. If they do, it must mean, I think, that birds realise that flats with a Southern aspect may get unbearably hot in summer.

Daffodils seem exceptionally good this year. The cold seems to suit them and, of course, makes them last much longer. We are particularly pleased with some white ones which we bought last autumn. I nearly made a fool of myself over them, however, because I did not know that when they first come out their trumpets are as yellow as a lemon. When the buds appeared, therefore, I wrote a powerful letter of complaint to the supplier, but luckily did not post it as I could not find the house's stamp. The next day the Daffodils were noticeably paler and after a day or two were all that the catalogue had claimed, thereby saving not only my blushes but a much more valuable fivepence.

The Doos take up Residence

1st May

The warm sunny spell we have been enjoying so much has gladdened the hearts of all of us. The Daffodils, which have been so good this year, are beginning to leave us and now need dead-heading every day. The trees are getting that fresh look of new green leaves. The birds welcome each new day with a crash of song, while cuckoos and others continue to sing about

them all the time. The village cherry trees are coming into
bloom and so once more our lovely valley slides peacefully into
the splendour of its spring. A truly wonderful time of year
which does more than compensate for all the rigours of the long
and arduous winter.

As if this were not enough we have had our other excitements
too. My wife's birthday coincided with a visit from grandchildren who gave her three white fan-tailed pigeons to live in
our new dovecote – sorry, 'doocot'. Graceful little creatures
who have already inveigled themselves into my wife's heart.

We were told that in order to persuade them to stay with
us they had to be shut up for a month or more, but the thought
of shutting them up for so long in this weather was more than
the family could bear. So an aviary was made with wire netting
and bamboo canes and an old fruit net which, when finished,
all agreed was only rivalled by that designed by Lord Snowdon
for the London Zoo. Unfortunately, in the general excitement
of the official opening one of the VIPs escaped and flew to the
top of a tall Wellingtonia, where, looking very pretty against
the blue of the sky, he watched the remainder of the proceedings
before flying back to Sussex whence he came.

We were comforted by being told that one of the three was
a trouble-maker and always fighting, and, as the remaining
two seemed to get on happily together, it is clear that it was the
trouble-maker who left us.

The two who are left, however, have chosen separate flats
(incidentally both facing South), which inclines me to think
that they are either two young gentlemen or two young ladies,
but this was such an unpopular suggestion that I refrained from
repeating it and accepted the explanation that it was because
they had probably not been introduced before they left.

Names were a matter of much debate and argument. My
own, as I thought, brilliant suggestion of 'Do' and 'Don't' was
received with the kindly respect to which grandfathers are
entitled, but never really got off the ground and was dismissed
as quickly as politeness would allow. Another suggestion
which found favour in my eyes was 'Bill' and 'Coo', but this

was also dismissed and could be disposed of a little more quickly as it came from one generation down. In the end we settled for 'Salt' and 'Pepper', I am not sure on what grounds but accepted the view of the youngest member of the committee that they were almost certainly the names that the two chiefly concerned would like best.

In addition to all these goings on, the Young Church Builders staged a Bring and Buy sale in the village hall, with a fancy dress parade in the middle of it thrown in for good measure, and from which the judges must have found it extremely difficult to pick the winner. But Miss Susan Pitman just won, dressed as Spring, wearing a frock decorated with all the spring flowers locally available, followed by Miss Jeanette Jones dressed as a Christmas cracker, and Trevor Mason as a Carpenter or, as the Bible more picturesquely puts it, 'a carver of wood and maker of cunning things' (tit boxes, perhaps, which were in notable demand at the sale).

Life, however, has also had its sombre moments. A meadow vole found his way into our greenhouse two nights ago and hewed down twenty-six of our forty-one cuttings of Carnations which were just about ready for potting, and trampled down almost all the labels so I don't know which are the survivors. But, with all the other breathless excitements going on, one fortunately has no time to brood.

It Was the Nightingale

17th May

Among the many pleasant things that happen all round us at this time of year has been the appearance of a nightingale who sings in the hedge at the back of our house. I had heard a snatch of a song from someone in that direction some time ago and it had crossed my mind that it might have been a nightingale but I decided that it was one of the warblers. A neighbour knowledgeable in these matters, however, has confirmed that it is a nightingale and told me that it is the first time that there has been one there for a number of years.

Unfortunately for us our bedroom is in the front of the house so we do not hear him at night and have to content ourselves with the sound of a passing car or motor bike speeding home in the early hours of the morning.

I suppose it does not matter much from the practical point of view whether one is woken up in the middle of the night by a motor bike or a nightingale. A motor bike, or at any rate one particular one in our vicinity, undoubtedly does the job more efficiently, so efficiently in fact that when it passes one positively leaps out of bed fully awake and wishing like the devil that the Russians or Americans would be more careful where they pointed their outer space rockets before they let them off, until one realises that it is only a bike and not a rocket and one creeps shamefacedly back into bed and goes to sleep again. A nightingale, of course, wakes one up much more gently, but on the other hand you do not go to sleep again so quickly because you lie awake a long time listening to him; so really it is as broad as it is long, but I suspect that most of us prefer the nightingale.

Nightingales or not, there is still the feeling about that spring has but a precarious hold. We have had so very few of those warm wonderful days when great lumps of curling cumulus clouds trundle slowly across the background of the sky while a hot sun shines down on the blossom and on the new green of the trees. Some of the trees, notably the oaks, are still in bud and the willows across the valley are still tipped with pink. Fledgeling birds seem fewer than usual at this time of year. House martins too seem fewer and for the first time since we have been here there is no sign of a pair building on our house, though I suppose there is still time for them to start. Only one snipe so far drums across the water meadows at the bottom of our garden in the evenings and the lapwing's call is rare. It was, of course, a late autumn and leaves were still on the trees well into November, but can it be that the seasons are slipping back and things happen a week or two later than they used to do fifty years ago?

One thing that does not appear to change is the weeds which grow as fast and as strongly as ever. Couch grass is one of our particular hates. Books tell us that the cure is to dig up and burn. I was discouraged to find this week, when part of a steep bank in our garden was cut into, that the roots of our local brew of couch went down into the ground as deep as five feet eight inches. It seemed a lot of trouble in order to produce two six-inch blades of grass and I could not help wondering what was the point of it all.

June Comes in Sunnily

The month of May seems to have slipped by unnoticed while we were still waiting for it, but we start June with the countryside looking its lovely best and with a heavenly day with big white clouds and a warm sun. The sort of day for which we all long and seem to expect as a right at this time of year but which is, when one comes to think of it, not all that common.

The hawthorn is in its full glory and some of the trees seem carved out of the local chalk, so thick is the blossom. It is a good year for blossom and as May produced no frightening frosts it should be a splendid year for fruit. Our own young trees certainly look as if they are going to bear fruit on a worthwhile scale for the first time. This may be because not only are they now getting comfortably established, but also perhaps because we have taken fruit trees more seriously and on expert advice have bought a few more which should be suitable mates for those which we already have. Even our fig tree now in its third year has two small figs about the size of peas which we are carefully nurturing for someone who, no doubt, will have a go at them just before they are ripe for picking.

Be all that as it may, we spent a happy and argumentative afternoon rigging our fruit cage and mending the holes in the netting so meticulously that it will be almost impossible for the birds to get out again without someone spending a frustrating half hour or so trying to drive them up into a corner where they can be captured and released outside.

Yesterday I had a curious and for me a unique experience. I came across a dead mole lying on his back on our lawn. He had only been dead a short time as the body was still warm. I examined him extremely carefully for any marks of violence, thinking that a cat which I saw hunting round that area a short time ago might have got him, but I could find no sign. So far as I know there has been no poison used thereabouts, but even if there had been one would have thought it most unlikely that he would come up to the surface to die or that he would roll over on his back to do so. It remains, therefore, one of those unsolved mysteries one would dearly like to know about. I am afraid that I still suspect the cat.

I am finding it difficult to write this letter because I am writing it, as I so often do when weather permits, out of doors by the river and am fascinated by watching a moorhen looking after her three newly-hatched chicks. The chicks could only have hatched out in the last couple of days because it is the first time that I have seen them, though I knew their nest. All three are quite at home swimming about or making voyages of discovery on to the lawn and scuttling back to the river at the first sign of anything that they do not quite like the look of. One is evidently the favourite child as, when the mother finds a particularly juicy morsel, she runs over and gives it to him, and I have just seen her swim two or three yards with what looked like a caterpillar in her beak and put it down his throat. The other two never seem to get a look in but in fact are quite capable of looking after themselves. So indeed is the favourite child. A few minutes ago he ran away when he saw his mother coming but was quickly overtaken and made to eat something whether he liked it or not and it seemed to me that he didn't as she had quite a struggle to make him take it.

So many fishermen who have known him over the years wanted to wish Mr Mott good luck on his retirement as Head River Keeper that the Leckford Estate gave a party to give them a chance to do so, and to which about a hundred people came. A notable tribute to someone who over the years has never spared himself to help others enjoy this lovely valley in which he himself was born and knows so well.

Summer in Her Stride

So far this must be one of the best Junes we have had for a very long time. Until today there has been warm unbroken sunshine and even now we are told by the experts that the spell will return this evening, so one does not grudge the warm soft drizzle that the garden is so eagerly lapping up.

The garden and countryside are settling quietly down to maturity. The wild excitement of the coming of the summer has eased up. Birds busy about gathering food for their families, have less time to sing, the fear of frost and of sudden and unexpected flurries of snow has gone. The cuckoo starts to stammer and summer steps gracefully into her stride. When June does her best and behaves as she has done so far there can be no more beautiful place in the world than England's green and pleasant land.

The moorhen about whom I wrote a fortnight ago has deserted her family, who now fend for themselves, and has started another. Whereas her first nest was carefully hidden away in the reeds, the new one is as conspicuous as could be, built in the middle of our carrier not two yards from the bank. This morning it has its sixth egg so I imagine she will now start what must be the boring chore of hatching them.

Two of our new pigeons are also busy sitting but one whom we call Salt insists, in an attempt perhaps to relieve the boredom, on keeping one egg in one corner and the other in another and divides her attention between them. I cannot believe that this method is likely to be a success but I suppose if you were a pigeon you might think it worth while giving it a try. Pepper, the other mother-to-be, prefers conventional methods and keeps her two together in a little nest of wood shavings.

In order to keep them with us we give our pigeons a small feed of maize and peas each afternoon and I was pleasantly surprised to find how quickly they became tame. When we first let them out they flew on to the roof of the house whenever we drew near, but it only took them a fortnight to learn to take food from our hands. There is a large fat wood pigeon who drops in regularly for tea. If he were not such a nuisance in the garden I would like to see how long it would take to make a friend of him too and am pretty certain that it could be done in a few weeks.

Peas are not so popular as the maize and quite a few get left on the lawn and are now sprouting vigorously. It is a contrary world. When we plant peas in the kitchen garden we soak them in paraffin, we spray the ground with evil smelling rodent repellent, we cover the lot with wire netting, set cunning traps for the unwary, scatter the ground yellow with slug pellets and build fluttering devices that one would think would frighten the daylights out of a myopic ostrich. But no sooner have we completed our last line of defence than word gets round and every form of mollusc, mammal and bird comes creeping, scampering and hopping from all over the county and with tooth, claw and beak seeks what it may devour – which is invariably our first sowing of peas. On the other hand, scatter a few peas on the open lawn with the express intention of feeding the hungry, and they lie there undisturbed until they have sprouted and grown to a size when they hamper the mowing machine.

After the Fête

On the 28th June we held our Annual Church Fête and we were all amazed how quickly it had come round again. This year there were no worries about the weather and all went according to plan in spite of the usual plethora of crises which reduced some members of the weaker sex to a couple of aspirins and some of the stronger to a quick visit to the Peat Spade in order to steady the nerves.

However, hard work and pulling together and generous last-minute volunteering overcame all crises, even the near failure of any strawberries to arrive in time, the sudden call of haymaking which nearly wrecked the Bowling for a Pig, and the near complete failure of the soft drink stall which by tradition has always been run by a lady who by some still inexplicable breakdown in communications failed to receive the message that the organising committee hoped that the long tradition would be maintained.

The younger members of the village distinguished themselves by collecting more money than in any previous year and wheedled sixpences and threepences out of their less quick-witted elders by persuading them, with a patter of sales talk that any practised confidence man would envy, to knock over tins, hit the rat, hammer a nail into a piece of wood and try other devices which looked easy but which were in fact impossible for anyone over the age of twelve.

Now that it is all over many of us are trying to catch up on the arrears of work that is to be done in the garden. The splendid spell of fine warm growing weather has made things grow so quickly that it has made it very difficult to keep up to date. Added to which various forms of vertebrates seem to have taken advantage of our preoccupation with other matters and have returned to harass us.

One of our moles has learnt a new trick which I must admit

I admire for its ingenuity but which I find disquieting as he might show others how to do it. Irritated, I suppose, by having to burrow round the traps that I lay for him, he now pushes up the trigger plate in a way that jams the jaws open and allows him to trot back and forth without let or hindrance.

I was told yesterday that the rat and mouse population round here has increased so much that it is now becoming a serious problem. I have not noticed it myself but I certainly shot two rats last week which were loitering round our new dovecote with, I suspect, intent to commit a felony. More serious, however, was the sight of two very small rabbits who, if not roaring like lions, were at any rate prowling round seeking what they might devour. I had thought that I had got rid of the rabbits in that part but evidently missed one pair. Catching sight of them unexpectedly round a flower bed, I suffered that same sudden shattering spasm of despair as one feels when one lets the Sellotape flip back on its roll.

Other menaces are the blackbirds. Like all of us, I love their song and am prepared to pay them fair wages for singing to us, but not at the price of *all* our strawberries and *all* our raspberries. However, nuisance as they are at times, it would be a dull world without them all and there are compensations such as when a badger comes to live not a hundred yards away. I have not seen him myself yet but Captain Burnett, one of my neighbours, tells me that he has. I am looking forward to meeting him and from what I am told I don't believe that badgers do much harm beyond digging up and eating a few bulbs.

Joys of Discovery

It rains as I write and no one seems to grudge it. It is not often during an English summer that one can say that. Almost all the hay is in, Wimbledon is over, the garden needs it and it is quite a change. Surely already this has been a summer to remember.

Certainly the country is looking lovely, the hedges full of dog roses and the hum of bees, the edges of the lanes white with cow parsnip and sprinkled with buttercups, but even so a poor showing compared with what they were half a century ago.

Mrs Mott, our postmistress, was telling me the other day that when she was a child there was a competition for children at the Church Fête, the winner being the child who could produce the biggest number of different wild flowers picked in the parish. She told me that she remembers winning it one year with well over thirty different kinds all picked in the lane that runs up past the church to the road that passes Danebury Hill. It would be interesting to see how many different kinds one could pick today, and if I can find the time I mean to try, but I don't think that it can be anything like so many.

It is, of course, the same with other forms of wild life. The everyday sights of one's childhood are no longer seen. Since we have lived here now over seven years, I have not seen a frog, a red squirrel, a toad, a grasshopper or even, I think, a cricket, and of course butterflies are comparatively few and far between, even the Cabbage White which in those far off days was so very common and at times a plague.

Even in an area such as this, where the land is intensely commercialised and farmed as efficiently as anywhere, it seems strange that so big a change should come about in so short a time, especially when we have the advantage of water meadows which up to now have remained more or less unexploited.

In spite of this, however, there is still plenty left to hold the interest of ordinary people who have no expert knowledge. In many ways perhaps one scores over the expert by not knowing too much. One is constantly discovering something new which the expert has known for years and for whom the discovery is ordinary and hardly worth bothering about. I noticed only the other day some marsh bedstraw in the water meadows. There is plenty of it about and I must have passed bits of it hundreds of times and yet because, I suppose, it is similar to so many other common straggly plants with clusters of small white flowers, I had never noticed it particularly before and got just as great a kick out of it when I ticked it off in my copy of *Fitch's Illustration of the British Flora* as any famous botanist discovering a plant hitherto unknown to natural science.

I like to look back too on the wonder and excitement of a very small relation who brought me a daisy from the lawn and who found that its discovery had not been recorded in the book. Now Bellis Perrenis is entered on page 126 proudly with her initials and date and place of discovery for all to see down through the ages.

I wish I could find the names of plants by the proper method. It should, of course, be quite easy to do but needs a fair amount of concentrated study which I am not prepared to give when there are so many other pressing things to do such as removing from among the strawberry beds large quantities of Senecio Vulgaris (discovered by M. J. F. Longstock, 7th August 1967) and Aegopodium Podograria (discovered by me daily) from anywhere in the garden where one cares to look.

Times Are What They Were

29th July

When one has retired and has nothing to do, it is astonishing how very little time one has in which to do it.

In my last letter I wrote how years ago there used to be a competition during our Church Fête to see how many different kinds of wild flower a child could gather in the parish and how I meant to try for myself how many I could find in the same lane from which Mrs Mott, when a child, once picked the winning bunch with well over thirty different kinds. I wrote that it seemed unlikely that today one could pick nearly so many.

I have not had time to try and it is now several weeks too late to make a fair comparison; so, like so many other things, it will have to wait until next year and take its place among the accumulated things that one wants to do.

The other day, however, we found that we had four or five minutes to spare on our way to lunch with friends in Wiltshire and stopped in a lane on the edge of Salisbury Plain to enjoy the view of the plain stretching away in the distance beyond the cornfield. While I was there I remembered the competition and looked to see what I could find near where I was standing. It was an interesting collection headed, for me at any rate, by a large stalk of yellow and brown flowers which I had to look up when I got home and found to be Broomrape. There were some fascinating little Pyramid Orchids, some Bugloss making a vivid patriotic splash among some Poppies and Daisies, Ladies' Bedstraw, Scabious and, of course, Dandelions, Knotweed, Thistles and Cow Parsnip, etc. So there were at least a dozen or so different kinds to be found without moving. It made me think that perhaps when writing last week I had fallen into the same old trap for so many of us in thinking that times are no longer what they were. I have for some years now noticed that policemen are getting younger and younger and have even begun to notice that the same thing is happening to police sergeants, so I should have heeded the warning and known better.

There are some things, however, that neither change with time nor alter with age. One day this week we heard a great disturbance going on in the garden. Blackbirds were clinking away like smithies, our pigeons, in an obvious state of agitation, were flying to our neighbour's roof, their place of refuge in times of trouble, other birds were making a fuss and even the moorhens were giving authoritative squawks to rally their young and take them to some hidden fastness in the reeds.

A few weeks ago this would have meant a squirrel in the trees was making his presence felt and, although I had got rid of that one, I thought perhaps another had come to take his place or perhaps a cat. I looked out of the window and there I saw a sizeable snake wriggling unhurriedly across the lawn, quite indifferent to the commotion and dismay that he was spreading for fifty yards around him. He disappeared into a flower bed and I saw him no more. He is, of course, quite harmless to human beings and to anyone else much larger than a small frog, but it is interesting how, in spite of this, down through the ages none of us, however big we are, likes a snake and start taking avoiding action and making a fuss whenever he appears.

Unpleasant though he is, he at any rate makes a good excuse for not weeding that particular bed for a bit. Not, of course, that one will ever have time to do it this year.

Time Running Out

4th August

The rain which arrived here a few days ago was both moderate and welcome but it broke the halcyon spell of hot days which has made this such a splendid summer and it also made us realise once more that good things do not last for ever.

The whole general look of the countryside is showing that time is passing all too quickly. In the last few days the fields of corn have turned a deeper shade of golden brown and look nearly ready for the combines. The reeds in the water meadows are beginning here and there to get that greyish look that tells that summer is on the wane. Small details confirm the general picture such as clusters of bright orange red berries on the Lords and Ladies standing out so vividly in shady places and this morning I noticed a pair of Hedge Brown butterflies fluttering round a blackberry bush in the lane.

The birds hardly sing at all, resting I suppose after the arduous duties of bringing up their families, though the house martins on our garage are still hard at work; also I found a pair of greenfinches trapped this morning in our greenhouse and so I imagine that being together they too are still foraging for a family. Greenfinches, I believe, are among those who go on nesting late. Mr Burtenshaw tells me that a pair of kestrels are still nesting in a tall tree at the bottom of his garden, but on the whole nesting is over.

One of the products of the nesting season in our little bit of the world is a very young robin hardly out of the fledgeling stage, with a speckly waistcoat only just beginning to turn colour and at the moment more pale orange than red. He looks as if he may become a friend this winter when he grows up, as he is always full of insatiable curiosity about everything we do in the garden.

I hope that he survives the many perils that beset small robins and all other young wild life at this time of year. Not only have they to survive the natural hazards of the wild, but the roads take a tremendous toll these days. Hardly a day passes that I do not see some young bird lying in the road killed by a passing car.

As I write this letter telling of the passing of the summer I am beginning to feel a horrid sensation in the pit of my stomach caused by the realisation that a large number of things will never get done which are on my list so boldly headed THINGS TO BE DONE and hung up prominently in our garden room where I cannot fail to see it several times a day. Hitherto I have been able to look it in the face without too many qualms, though admittedly thinking to myself that it is time that I got on with some of them; but 'Bed out Asters', which is second on my efficient organisation list, has now become an affront. I have not got round to sowing them yet and the packet of seeds still lies unopen on my desk. I must procrastinate no longer. After all the secret of good gardening is efficient organisation. It is time that I made another list. I will do it tomorrow.

About Predators

25th August

We were sitting having tea by the river when a sparrow hawk flew up from the valley and perched high up in a willow tree at the bottom of the garden.

When we have tea in the garden I nearly always have a pair of field glasses handy so that I can see what anybody is up to, so I had a very good view of her. She was a very handsome creature with her bright yellow legs and brown and white chest, sitting bolt upright. She sat there for a long time preening herself but otherwise doing nothing much.

After a few minutes a moorhen came out of the reeds followed by her three young ones, now rapidly growing up and already showing little white patches on their tails. The mother came out on to the lawn while the young ones just swam about nibbling at anything worth nibbling at.

Suddenly the hawk swooped down off the tree and made straight for them. The moorhen on the lawn must have seen her out of the corner of her eye for she let out a loud shout of warning and ran as hard as she could to the bank. It was quite unlike the usual sound she makes when alarmed and was exactly as if she had suddenly shouted 'Look out!' The three young ones obviously knew what it meant as all three immediately dived and swam under water to the shelter of the reeds and I never saw them come up.

The hawk went back to her perch on the tree and went on waiting. A few minutes later she swooped down again, this time right down into the reeds about twenty yards away where I lost sight of her but she came up again very quickly carrying nothing, so I suppose she missed whomever it was she was after, and then flew off to try her luck elsewhere.

It was an interesting and exciting ten minutes. I was glad the moorhens escaped, but why I don't know. Hawks, after all, have to live and bring up a family the same as anyone else. I suppose it is because we have watched the moorhens grow from the time they were eggs and so take a proprietary interest in them and also perhaps because a human's sympathy is always with the young and small, but this feeling seems peculiar to man. It is certainly not the case with hawks or other birds or animals except where their own young are concerned.

The hot summer has been ideal for wasps who are now so plentiful that they are a nuisance. Their arrival here coincided with the arrival of grandchildren and made a lively combination. Breakfast seems to go something like this: 'Go away Wasp' – 'Well don't send him over here' – 'zzzzzzzzz' – 'Look out!' – 'Don't do that. Let him settle' – 'Mind Grandfather's coffee' – 'Damn' – 'Darling!' – 'Sorry, darling, but . . .' – 'Oh, sorry Grandfather' – 'Fetch a cloth somebody' – 'zzzzz' – 'Keep still everyone' – 'Now quickly' – 'Got him' – 'Please may I kill the next one I've invented a patent way' – 'Pass the wasp – I mean the marmalade, please' – 'zzzzzzzzz' – 'Don't *do* that' – 'zzzzz' – 'Look out!' and so on. Not very good for the digestion perhaps but much less harmful to it than reading the papers.

Mysterious Goings On

1st September

And so September. The great field over on the other side of the valley, which we have watched grow gradually from green to yellow and on to corn, has suddenly turned brown again under the plough. How one hates to see the summer leave, especially this one which has been so generous. Yet September can so often be a lovely month that one cannot help but give it a welcome, more nervous perhaps than grudging.

One of the nicer things about September so far as we are concerned is the arrival of the small pink Cyclamen (Neapolitan) which pop up suddenly out of the ground without waiting for their leaves. We planted a small patch of them under some trees a few years ago and they have settled and now make a very pretty patch of colour. Like Columbines they have the extra charm of looking as beautiful in the mass as they do when looked at close to individually. Encouraged by the summer they are much earlier this year and some have been in flower for a week or two. We were particularly pleased to see them as for some reason or other the place where they were planted was earlier in the year a very favourite one for rabbits, who were continually making their scrapes there and digging up the corms.

Mysterious other scrapes still appear here and there but I am fairly certain that they are not made by rabbits as I have not seen one for months and think that the few that there were have succumbed once more to myxomatosis. A friend has told me that they look like scrapes made by a badger and she may well be right as there is said to be one living under some trees quite close.

Another mystery is the sudden disappearance of a small plant which was given me by a friend in Ireland from his garden who asked me if I could find out its name as none of his neighbours could help him. I planted it in one of our beds, meaning to ask one of the local experts what it was when it got a bit bigger and flowered and then, blow me down, someone came in the night and, ignoring all else, nibbled it right down so that it was not there any more.

Our pigeons too have suddenly become very nervous and no longer come near us at feeding time, whereas two or three of them used to fly up and eat out of our hands. Two of them disappeared for a couple of days altogether, so there seems to be something sinister going on. If one had the energy it would be interesting to sit up on a moonlight night in the garden and watch. I am sure that a great deal more goes on than one thinks.

When I was a young man in India I sometimes sat up all night in the jungle watching what was happening and found it quite fascinating. As soon as night fell the whole area seemed to come much more alive with the air full of squeaks and rustlings and then at intervals suddenly complete silence as if some sudden danger threatened, which it probably did.

Meantime, however, there is plenty enough to see during the day and this week over the pond we had the luck to see on several occasions a magnificent dragonfly, one of the largest I have ever seen, shining like a turquoise and yellow jewel. I tried to name it from Miss Longfield's book *The Dragonflies of the British Isles*, but not very successfully. I finally stumped for Somatachlora Metallica, said to be a rare British species. It is a nice name anyhow and if I can remember it I will trot it out nonchalantly when talking to friends and expect I shall get away with it as I don't suppose anyone except Miss Longfield will know any better.

Blackberry Harvest

15th September

We have been away for the inside of a week staying with relations in Sussex and very much enjoying two or three hot sunny days when, from what we have been told, it was dull, drizzly and cold here all the time. We were, after all, only in the next county yet the difference was evidently very marked and goes to show the variety of the English climate.

It was a happy visit. The house where we stayed was in the middle of a farm and they brought in the last of the best harvest they had had for years on the evening that we arrived. As our hostess remarked, we were surrounded by an atmosphere of contented achievement, with the barns full of corn and the men's pockets full of well-earned overtime and everybody bronzed, healthy and happy.

Whatever the reasons, we also felt the atmosphere and returned home full of happy achievement in the form of a harvest of fifteen pounds of the best blackberries that I have seen for many a long day. We were surprised to find what a good crop it was in spite of the dry summer and I think that they must be some variety peculiar to the district.

There were stretches where the bushes grew thick and low and where the fruits were fat and juicy with each individual drupe black and shiny and almost the size of an elderberry. So juicy in fact that they soaked through the bottom of one of the bags they were in and spilled out on to the garage floor as I lifted them out of the car.

However they were soon scraped up with a trowel that was luckily handy and are now as I write boiling on the kitchen stove half way through their metamorphic journey to jelly. Happily I have been unable to trace so far, among the delicious fumes arising from the big bubbling pot, the slightest whiff of motor grease or petrol or even of the Chrysanthemum fertiliser for which the trowel was last used.

Among other important events that have happened while we were away has been the arrival of contractors who painted the inside walls of the church, making it look resplendent and, as our vicar aptly put it, 'like a little cathedral'. Even our Honorary Treasurer, who has been known to say that the only colours worth considering when it comes to decorating are black and red, went so far as to announce that it did not seem to look so bad after all.

It was, I gather, a near run thing whether the church would be ready for early service on Sunday but, thanks to a small band of volunteers who spent much of Saturday scrubbing, cleaning and polishing, it was done.

So what with the rota of ladies who do the flowers each week, and with the brass kept so polished by Miss Child, our organist, that it would break the spirit of any Master at Arms in the Royal Navy who might try to fault it, and the altar linen hand laundered by Mrs Hatcher, the wife of our new Vicar's Warden, our church must be one of the best cared for in the diocese.

Autumnal Glow of Achievement

The dead leaves are beginning to cover the lawn to an extent that is becoming unacceptable and it looks as if sweeping them up cannot be much longer delayed. Our Sweet Peas, which were still flowering here and there, have had to make way for spring cabbages and the compost heap grows larger every day with rubbish from all the beds.

Foggy mornings hold back the early-morning sun and when it clears the meadows glisten with foggy dew on the spiders' webs so that even the most dim-witted fly, using only a mere half dozen of his eyes, could not fail to recognise them and take heed. It is no use pretending any longer that winter is not preparing to march; but it has been a most wonderful summer for all of us, so even a spider has no right to complain.

For us it has been exceptionally exceptional. We have at last achieved a melon. Not one but two and a half. We ate our first one today for lunch. It was admittedly a bit hard in places but not so hard that one could not cut it with an ordinary table knife and it was deliciously sweet when sugared enough. The other still sits in the linen cupboard and seems to be making good progress as every day the bit round the stalk, when pressed hard with a thumb nail, seems to yield a bit more. The half melon we have had to abandon. It was only the size of a golf ball anyway so we do not mind much. It has taken six years of work, study and research to produce this crop, but after lunch we felt that it had all been very much worth while.

Our other achievement this year has been a peach. About six years ago we planted out a tiny seedling an inch or two high sprouting from a peach stone which Mrs Emery, who lives down the road, had saved from her husband's dinner and had given us. It grew strongly and as straight as a ram rod, as might be expected from anyone who had once done duty on the dinner plate of Mr Emery, who is a retired sergeant of the Royal Marines.

Various experts from time to time had shaken their heads sadly over it and had told us that we were wasting our time and that we had far better use the space for something else, but we persevered, until this year for the first time it produced a large and handsome fruit.

Brimming over with excitement and a sense of achievement, my wife spent a large part of the morning of its discovery describing the phenomenon to a friend while they were doing their duty turn of delivering meals on wheels to elderly people round about. She returned, I thought, a little deflated as her friend, who owns a large and beautiful garden nearby and who is herself a keen and expert gardener, did not seem to be much impressed and eventually told her that in horticultural circles it had been known for a very long time now that peaches grew on peach trees, which, after all, is true enough I suppose if one comes to think of it.

An Encounter with Dasychira Pudibunda

13th October

On a hot afternoon last week we found, walking across our lawn towards the river, a most wonderful caterpillar. He is, I have learned since, fairly common but I had not seen his like before and was duly impressed. He had a shiny jet black skin which was clothed in pale yellow and light pea-green segments like little rounds of quilting and covered in light ginger hairs. On each of his first four segments nearest his green face there was a small tuft of rust-coloured hair so thick that it looked like fur, and then, to crown all, on the last segment there was a rich crimson tail made of hairs about a quarter of an inch long and sticking straight up like the tail of a pleased dog.

When I picked him up he rolled himself into a flat ring looking for all the world like a piece of modern jewellery but prettier, so I tucked him away safely under some bushes in a flower bed lest some bird took a fancy to him.

I was so intrigued with him that I wrote to the manager of the moth and butterfly department at the Natural History Museum to learn more about him because I thought that so magnificent a little person must turn into an equally magnificent something which would be nice to see flying around.

I got a charming hand-written letter back saying that from the description I gave he was probably the caterpillar of the Pale Tussock Moth (Dasychira Pudibunda) and I was also told what he ate in case I wanted to keep him. As, however, the letter went on to say that the adult moth was only a rather drab grey, I did not think keeping him would be worth while. Also, feeding four pigeons is difficult enough to arrange and to add a caterpillar seemed likely to strain the organisation to breaking point. Besides I have no wish to turn the garden into a sort of junior Whipsnade; there are too many important things to do – sweeping leaves for instance.

I happened to mention our encounter with the caterpillar to Sir Bernard Miller who told me that by a coincidence he too had met one of the same tribe on the golf course on the same day and furthermore he had met the only other one of its kind that he had ever seen almost exactly a year ago in almost exactly the same place.

We tried to look him up in a book he had on moths and butterflies but could not find him. However I learned that I need not have bothered about hiding him away out of sight because we read that no bird except a cuckoo will touch a really

hairy caterpillar because the hairs stick in the gullet and stifle
it. Cuckoos apparently will try anyone once, even those with a
green face, a shiny jet black skin, wearing four pale green
fur-trimmed overcoats in a row with a crimson tail sticking up
behind.

It might interest readers to know that the Museum also sent
me a list of relevant books, societies, names and addresses of
butterfly nurseries and of an entomological bookseller; in fact
it could not have been more helpful. In these days when people
are discussing the problem of how to use increased leisure, it is
encouraging to realise how much museums are ready to help
those who want to know more about small everyday matters.

Colours of a Saintly Summer

25th October

I have had to be away being hospitalised, or should one say
away hospitalising? (I am not very well up in modern English
usage, and Fowler doesn't help), so have been out of touch
with all the important things that have been going on in
Longstock this last fortnight. This letter, therefore, must
necessarily be brief and readers, if any, must content themselves
with reading only about what has been going on in the world
outside such as civil wars among Arabs, football fans, Ulster-
men, Vietnamese and West Africans, not to mention possibilities
of a snap general election, world disarmament before there is
so much armament that there will not be enough world to use
it all on, and richly rewarded biographies of ladies who have
lived luxuriously on the criminal activities of their husbands or

on less criminal but equally undesirable activities of their own and other exciting happenings which seem always to pass Longstock by.

I also had the misfortune to miss the wonderful spell of record warm weather that the Saints Luke and Martin together with India must have all combined to give us and which is even now continuing. A truly wonderful summer it has been from June onwards. Alas it has gone so quickly that one seems to have had only enough time to enjoy a small part of it as day after day it rushed by. Except for a day or two here and there we have not been away from home this summer at all and we wonder how and where the days have gone and wish so much that we could drag them back and have them all over again more slowly. For some, perhaps, unhappily this has not been so, but even in their cases the lovely summer must have helped them face their difficulties and disappointments more bravely.

I returned to find little change in the garden, the crop of crab apples a bit more crimson, the scattered Dogwoods in the water meadows opposite a bit more yellow and the Liquidamber, which has grown this year so much bigger, turning a soft reddy bronze. Our Dahlias disappeared a month ago in an early frost which killed them but spared our neighbours', but we are still left with lots of Roses and other bits of colour left over from the summer to which autumn tints are adding.

The only disappointment is the disappearance of another pigeon whose wife, I am ashamed to say, ran off with a stranger some time ago. I hope an owl has not got him. I heard one very early this morning hooting very loudly and much nearer than usual. In fact it sounded as if he might have been perched on the top of the dovecote itself but it was too dark to see. If he had been it must have been terrifying to the inhabitants and quite enough to hospitalise all of them.

The Convenience and Charm of a Strong Nor-Wester

For the past two days great westerly winds have been ripping the leaves off the tops of the trees and scattering them as far as the river. Even those which had already fallen some days before were sent leaping and scampering across the lawn as if death and dying were the most exciting things imaginable. Fascinating as it was to watch, one could not help feeling some despondency as one realised that so much scatteration was making the task of sweeping them all up so much more difficult.

Today all is changed; the gale has blown itself out and we are left with one of those quiet autumn days with a hot sun low in the sky shining on the red and golden leaves. The air so still that as one sweeps one can hear the distant murmur of village voices mingling with the sound of rooks in the trees three fields away. As I was sweeping, our robin, as full of curiosity as ever, perched on the branch of a tree not ten feet away to watch and sing. He looked so pretty sitting in the very small patch of sunlight in which he chose to sing his song that it made boredom impossible.

Tomorrow perhaps the forecasted north-westerlies will come; always particularly welcome here at this time of year because they blow the leaves away from the garden and into the fields and the harder they blow the more welcome they become, especially as they so often bring sunshine with them.

Apart from this local convenience, strong north-westerly winds have, for me at any rate, a charm of their own. It may be because some of the finest sailing I have ever enjoyed has been done on their wings. I once breakfasted in the Helford River and dined at Camaret well over a hundred miles away on the same day in a friend's yacht, fizzing across the channel in bright sun with a strong north-westerly up our tail hardly touching a sheet the whole way across.

Another sail I shall always remember in similar conditions is when we came on watch to find a big sea running in the early morning sun. As the watch wore on the wind freshened and conditions became so exhilarating that it was almost too late before I realised that we were carrying more sail than was prudent and I remember the helmsman having a very anxious ten minutes or so while two of us worked to get sail off her before something parted or we broached to. Lamentable seamanship admittedly, but hissing down those great streaky valleys of the seas sparkling in the sun one forgot about prudence and merely felt like standing up and shouting one's head off just for the pure joy of being there.

Elderly leaf-sweepers can hardly expect to recapture those moments of wild excitement from watching a strong nor-wester blowing leaves away from a lawn but they can get a great deal of quiet satisfaction from it all the same.

On Sunday the village held its usual Remembrance Day service round the War Memorial in bright sun between heavy showers of rain. The church itself, as always, was beautifully decorated with flowers from people's gardens, but someone this week had filled the altar vases with small dark evergreens mixed with Remembrance Day Poppies with a few slender sprays of white Snowberries falling down like tears, symbolising so simply the feelings of so many.

Sensitive Plants

Not along ago I was discussing with an American friend the possibility that plants have feelings. There are, after all, plants that trap flies and other insects for food and digest them with similar juices to those used by everyone else. This seems to me to be quite a step towards becoming a sensate being. I was interested, therefore, to receive the other day from my friend a cutting from the San Francisco Chronicle saying that the Backster Research Foundation of New York has been experimenting on these lines and apparently considers that it is likely to be true.

A friend and near neighbour of ours grows extremely good Lilies on which she is very keen, but tells us that she is always very jealous of a friend who always grows much better ones no matter where she happens to be. When asked how she manages to do it she answered quite seriously that she treats them as friends and goes out to see them every day to talk to them and generally fuss over them but never bothers to give them any special treatment or fertiliser or anything of that sort.

There is, of course, the corollary of this the other way when we read about the fig tree in the Bible which was cursed because it bore no fruit and withered away.

Mr Duncan, the Director of Gardening at Longstock House, told me that it used to be quite common practice among old-fashioned professional gardeners when they found that a plant was not doing well to pot it up and carry it round with them and put it down next to them wherever they were working and even take it back to their homes at night until it got better.

I cannot say that my own experience has been very encouraging. I tried speaking very civilly for a change to one of our Carnations who produces silly shaped blooms but it never took the slightest notice. Nevertheless the whole idea may not be so far fetched as would at first appear. Knowledge is growing at such a tremendous pace in these computer days that almost any idea cannot be dismissed as being impossible.

Another idea that we were discussing was that some insects can talk. It will not be long now, if it has not already been invented, before there will be some sort of microscope for sound which will be able to sort out almost inaudible sounds from the rest and magnify them so that one will be able to hear what goes on in, say, an ant's nest, so we may soon be able to know for certain.

It seems most unlikely that such an orderly and complex community as a swarm of bees or community of ants can organise itself without some very efficient form of communication. I am sure that if I were an ant I would find that a couple of antennae stuck in my nut would be hopelessly inadequate for finding my way about in the pitch dark, let alone enable me to perform the various complicated duties that each ant has to do for the good of the community.

It seems that it is now established that dolphins are able to talk to each other, so why not ants, who seem to be a great deal more sophisticated? It could, I suppose, be argued that if they can they would by now have talked themselves into living more comfortably than in an ant heap, but it would take a stronger argument than that to convince me that it is all nonsense.

Goings on in the Dovecote

The last of the leaves have fallen from the trees, which now stand black and bare ready to face the winter while waiting like the rest of us for spring. A professional gardener told me the other day that he could not remember a year when the leaves had been so many and sweeping them up had taken so long. Nor could I, but fear it is due to the increase in the number of one's years rather than any natural phenomenon of an increase in the number of leaves.

However, with the trees bare a broom or rake no longer feels like Mrs Partington's mop and one has had at last a spare moment in which to go round the garden and see what has been happening while one's back has been turned and almost bent double.

A quick inspection revealed that all was well and no major disaster had occurred in spite of quite a severe frost or two. I even found an occasional flower reminding us of the splendid summer that we had had and encouraging us to look forward to the next. One or two purple Pansies still survived and in the herbaceous border two thin small spikes of Delphiniums which I thought that the frost must have killed had revived and I even saw a blossom or two on the strawberry plants. Mice had so far not been able to break through the anti-mouse defences in order to devour the seedlings in the greenhouse, except only in one case where they must have brought their own scaling ladders or dropped down by parachute. In fact the only disturbing feature about the whole tour of inspection was the number of leaves that were lying about unswept.

Our white fan-tailed pigeons have recently been living through very agitating times and have made us realise that a flutter in the dovecote is no idle expression.

We were originally given three – Mustard, Pepper and Salt, and then a neighbour gave us four more. One of the four went straight home to Mum as soon as she was let out at the end of her three weeks' quarantine. Another got run over in the road a day or two later, leaving us with five. These lived happily together for most of the summer until a handsome young chap with a light brown body and a while tail arrived, who, in spite of my efforts to discourage him, called daily and made goo-goo eyes at one of the girls and eventually ran off with her, leaving us with four.

The fourth, presumably the outraged husband, tried to console himself with Salt, but was seen off by Mustard who was having no nonsense of that sort and was not prepared to part with Salt any more than he was with Pepper, so the outraged husband left us to find solace elsewhere.

Mustard, Pepper and Salt then settled down and lived happily until about a fortnight ago when the erring young wife re-appeared, having obviously been left in the lurch by her boyfriend, as anyone could have told her could only be expected from a chap with a light brown body and a white tail. Pepper and Salt, now respectable young matrons, were not having her back at any price and went for her whenever she got too near and especially when she started sidling up to Mustard.

We were wondering what would happen in the end when two days ago the outraged husband arrived and, although rather coldly received by everyone, was at last accepted and all seem now to have settled down again.

I would like to think that all has been forgiven and forgotten but I rather think that regular meals and a centrally heated flat (I have installed one of those small car-warming paraffin lamps in the dovecote) have rather more to do with it than they should.

Party Time

While those who live in small villages experience nothing of the tumult and hurly-burly of Christmas time in the big cities, they nevertheless come under its influence, though more gently and, many would think, in a more quiet and dignified way. It is certainly the case in Longstock.

Not that we do not enjoy ourselves, and perhaps quiet is not the right word. The decibel output per square foot, or minute, or however sound is scientifically measured, in the Village Hall during the children's Christmas party must compare competitively with the noise in Trafalgar Square at the height of the Christmas rush hour, or with the cheering crowds on the steps of St Paul's Cathedral at midnight on New Year's Eve, bells and all. Our rendering in church of 'Hark the Herald Angels Sing' must also take a lot of beating, especially the last high 'hark', which some of the older ones are beginning to find difficult to reach and consequently put in an extra spurt to help themselves achieve it.

The Women's Institute celebrated its golden jubilee also in the Village Hall, and, though it is coincidence that the date fell at this time of the year, the spirit of Christmas time undoubtedly added to the high spirits of the members who attended the party dressed in the fashions of fifty years ago and led by Mrs Goater, who is not only a founder member, but was a mature matron of over forty when she joined.

But perhaps the party that is not only enjoyed as much as any other by those taking part, but takes precedence in the hearts of many, is that of the Over 60's Club. Under the energetic organisation of Miss Druitt and Miss Warne, this Club is holding its Christmas party in the Village Hall next Tuesday.

There will be assembled representatives of a generation who have probably seen greater changes than any generation before

them. Survivors of two world wars who lived through shortages
and anxieties of not only the two great wars but of cruelly bad
times which happily the young have never had to face. Many of
them fought in the last war and one or two in the war before
as well – bombed, shelled and one at least torpedoed. A tough,
resilient and almost indestructible generation ready to face
calmly and resolutely anything that fate may hurl at them. The
children's brass band from the school is to play to them at tea.

1970

No End of Activities

The bitter weather has put an end to gardening but there have been plenty of other activities going on to keep us all occupied.

No less than fifty-two children came from the local school to play their brass band and sing to the Over 60's Club at its Christmas party. It was indeed spectacular proof of the population explosion, as the performers outnumbered the performees by a comfortable margin and overflowed from the stage on to the floor of the Village Hall and rather unfairly near, I thought, to the splendid spread of buns and cakes and jellies with which the over sixties were to be regaled at tea. One had complete confidence, however, in the young schoolmaster in command who controlled, seemingly without effort, about a dozen brass implements, big bass drums, several fiddles and fifty-two children with the lightest of light batons which really could only have been a magic wand in disguise.

On the 28th December we had our carol service in the church when our temporary vicar blessed the crib while the children stood round holding candles before making a candlelight procession up the aisle before the service began.

Another event in the village hall last week was the concert competition given by the children to raise funds for the church.

Each member of the audience was given a slip of paper on which to write down what they considered to be the order of merit of the performers. At the end of the concert these were handed to Mr Webster who retired to commune with a computer which he said he had installed behind the scenes.

After a few agonising minutes of anxious expectancy, he re-appeared to announce the winner to be Miss Caroline Burtenshaw, aged nine, for her rendering of Bach's Minuet in G. The win was all the more creditable and popular because this piece as it turned out was an unlucky choice; the reason being that the recent damp weather had got into the piano and, as bad luck would have it, made G of all notes very unreliable, needing a very hard thump and sometimes two to make it sound at all. Miss Burtenshaw, of course, could not have been expected to know this and it says much for her determination that, after a forgivable moment of shocked dismay when note G first failed to respond, she quickly acquired the knack and by the time she had reached the difficult last page was able to embark on it with almost as much self-confidence as if she had been Paderewski himself faced by the same awkward situation at some similarly important public recital.

As if all these excitements were not enough to keep us going, the Bishop of Winchester is coming next week to induct our new vicar into the parishes of Longstock and Leckford.

The Arrival of Snowdrops
and a New Vicar

12th January

A sprinkling of Snowdrops now show like little signposts that we are on the road to spring. Of all the signs of changing seasons the first Snowdrops seem to make the deepest impact. Why this should be so I find difficult to say. After all the first blooms of an incurved Chrysanthemum are a much more impressive sight and yet for all their magnificence they fail to stir the emotions to anything like the same extent or make one call to mind all the joys, sorrows, disappointments and dangers that one has experienced since one saw them last or raise such splendid hopes for the year to come before we see them again.

They seem to be late this year. Usually they start appearing at the beginning of January and I noticed that the small clump of them outside the church door, which are nearly always out on Christmas Day, are now only just in bud. There seems to be no general rule. This autumn, unlike last year's when many trees were still green in late October, did not seem to be particularly late but on the other hand Mr Mott told me the other day that he had noticed a large number of swallows flying about the village on 10th November which was far later than he had ever seen them before in the sixty odd years that he has lived here.

Mr Michel, our new vicar, was successfully inducted last week with all the pomp and ceremony that such an occasion warrants. The Bishop of Winchester in his full regalia, accompanied by the Archdeacon, the Rural Dean and neighbouring clergy and churchwardens were an impressive sight and helped to bring home to members of the parish that for half an hour or so our little church was as important in the scheme of things as Westminster Abbey on a state occasion.

The somewhat complicated and meaningful service was con-

119

ducted without a hitch, which was very creditable as the
rehearsal that had been arranged had had to be cancelled.

It had been arranged for an evening earlier in the week on
the day that Mr Michel and his wife and four children arrived
to live in the vicarage for the first time. It was a bitterly cold
night and blowing a blizzard. Just as the rehearsal was due to
start a pipe burst in the vicarage attic and put out all the lights
and cut off all means of cooking or heating. The main stopcock,
when eventually traced, was found to have seized up and could
not be closed so those officials and parishioners who had been
summoned to the rehearsal had therefore quickly to change
roles and spent the evening with buckets, mops and cloths
trying to stem the flood as it poured down the stairs and through
the ceilings, urged on and encouraged by the vicar's small son
who read them smashing jokes and super riddles from his
comic by the light of a failing electric torch.

It is reported that the vicar remarked the next morning how
fortunate he and his family had been that matters had not been
worse. A remark that has mystified one of his parishioners at
least ever since.

The Battle of the Carnations

2nd February

In spite of the wet the countryside and the gardens are
beginning slowly to wake up, but about a week to ten days
later than usual. I have a useful if sentimental yardstick by
which to measure this. Eight years ago I picked for a lady a
small bunch of snowdrops that I discovered tucked away on a

bank in the middle of a patch of scrubby Elm Suckers and nettles. In spite of my clearing away the rubbish and making various alterations, the Snowdrops have somehow survived and I have been able to pick for the same lady a small bunch of Snowdrops from the same patch on the 26th January of each year since then until this year when she has had to be content with two very small buds, which even so took a deal of finding.

Why this should be is difficult to say, for the winter, though wet, has been generally mild. I suspect that the very hard spell that we had for a few days after Christmas knocked back the early risers such as the Snowdrops and also the Winter Aconites which are now only beginning to show themselves.

Crocuses are pushing their way through normally and mice seem to have eaten fewer of ours than usual, which is lucky as our unfortunate neighbour lost all his in one night and called me over to see the scene of devastation. Each bulb, and there must have been a hundred or so, had been dug up and the young shoots bitten off and left lying on the ground. Another neighbour told me a similar story but had managed to save his from complete annihilation by drastic trapping. He also told me that his mice went for the specially good ones and left the ordinary hybrid ones alone. This may account for ours being spared as they are nearly all hybrids, but it may also be because when I planted them last autumn I gave each bulb a pinch of naphthalene alongside it. I fear, however, that the real reason is that they have been so busy eating our Carnations that they have not yet had time to get round to chewing our crocuses.

In the battle of Carnations I suffered a severe defeat, all the more humiliating because it was my own fault by getting too cocky. One should have learnt by now that small birds, mice, rabbits, moles, caterpillars, slugs, etcetera and etcetera exploit to the full the slightest error or negligence on one's own part and turn a minor setback into a complete rout if one does not keep one's head and immediately start fighting back every inch of the way.

I had noticed that a shoot on a Carnation had been nibbled

by an intruder and, suspecting mice, fought back by setting traps and inflicted a few casualties but not enough to act as a deterrent, so I hotted things up by resorting to poison and after a day or two felt that I had won. A few days later the enemy recovered sufficiently to launch a vicious counter attack which left a couple of plants shootless. I decided to fight back by cutting off the enemy's line of communication and spent some time crawling round the greenhouse reconnoitring and found a couple of holes in the wall through which were led the water pipe and the electric cable. These I blocked up with cement, and went on my way rejoicing and thinking how much better it was to be a man than a mouse.

It was here that I made the mistake that was to prove fatal. The idea, though brilliantly conceived and superbly executed, failed because I discovered when I returned to the scene three days later that I had blocked the enemy in instead of out. I have now no Carnations left worth talking about from which I can take cuttings.

Things are Stirring

After a week of warm wet slop and slush, winter has launched a savage attack which has sent us all scuttling to find another jersey before going out, and to the fireside after coming in; but, for all the bitter fierceness of the offensive our valley defies it with its beauty. The steel grey river, slowly gliding through the snow-covered water meadows with their fawn reeds and bare black trees under a shining pale blue sky, makes a scene of cold magnificence which fills one with chilly admiration and almost affection.

The birds, who only a few days ago were just beginning to feel that it was time to make plans for the spring, now spend much of their time low in the hedges searching for something to eat.

The scarcity of food has made the cock chaffinch, already gay in his spring colouring, who waits each morning for my wife to appear to replenish the bird table, more friendly than ever and it is a race between him and the robin as to who gets to her first long before she herself gets to the table. Both jump the queue by having titbits given to them privately before the doors are open to the general public. Even the starlings are now much bolder and my wife has to wait shivering by the bird table while the small ones first have their feed; otherwise the starlings come down and drive them off and leave nothing for the rest. There is no Oxfam organisation in the bird world.

Although the search for food dominates the thoughts of the birds and no doubt others such as the mice, rabbits and beetles (not to mention moles) who share our garden with us, there are signs that other important matters are beginning to be thought about. I notice that a few of the ducks who use our carrier at the bottom of the garden have already paired up, and on Sunday morning I saw two cock pheasants, with their brilliant plumage shining in the sun and snow, wandering about our lawn and then two hens appeared from under the trees and started walking towards them but modestly pretending not to notice where they were going. Whether they were two pairs or two unattached boys and girls just going for a Sunday walk, as unattached young people of the same sex are wont to do, I do not know. Nor could I wait to find out as the church bell changing its note told all dawdlers that they had no more time in which to linger, no matter what important discoveries they were on the brink of making.

One of our pigeons has made an early start and is sitting on two eggs in a most economical nest as all she has done is to place a few twigs across the corner of her one-roomed flat as a barrier to stop the eggs from rolling about. The last time she sat she did not bother, or did not know, about nests, with the result that the eggs used to roll about and get separated and, though she conscientiously gave each a turn of sitting, it was of course hopeless from the start. I think she must have thought out the twig idea for herself, as there has been no one to show her how to build a proper nest. Pigeons are evidently expected to build proper nests, otherwise their eggs would be much more pointed so that they cannot roll about – like those laid by birds such as the guillemot who lay them on ledges.

Our Snowdrops are now nearly at their best, but unfortunately are almost invisible against the snow, though one or two orange spikes of crocus buds are here and there peeping through to encourage us and bid us all have patience and stick it out a little longer.

Spring in the Bird World

At long last and quite suddenly the northerly winds, the snow and the rain have left us alone and for the past two days we have been allowed a taste of spring. As Mr Morse, our postman, remarked: 'It's been long enough coming to make sure it will do us all a bit of good.' It certainly has done the birds a bit of good and it is delightful to hear the excited twitterings and short bursts of song that are once again beginning to sound through our valley. It is all the more noticeable because up to two days ago it was comparatively silent.

Crows have started building at the very top of one of our elm trees where there are two nests side by side. Although there are as yet only two nests, there seem to be many more crows and I counted as many as seven yesterday all fussing round. On an elm the other side of the garden, also very high up, there are two pairs of jackdaws building and on the other side of the field next to us there is a small rookery, so we are becoming experts in Corvidae, especially as only last week, when we were down in Cornwall, I saw, for I think the first time in my life, a pair of wild ravens. They looked enormous and very fierce.

Seeing them reminded me that I had once been told that even in these days some East Coast mothers, in districts where the raven is rarely if ever seen, still threaten their children that if they are not good the black raven will come and carry them off. However, the saying does not refer to the bird but to the Vikings who painted a huge black raven on their sails.

Not being an ornithologist, it took me a long time to sort out the crows from the rooks and the jackdaws even with field glasses, but I think that I have now got them buttoned up. I am told that I should get rid of the crows, as they do much harm robbing the nests of small birds and sometimes eating the inhabitants, but I would be sorry to do so as they are interesting to watch and also I am one of those who like the noise they make.

I may, however, have to get rid of them because when my wife or I are not about they come down and help themselves to the food put out for the pigeons and I saw one yesterday bullying Salt, one of our pigeons who had a road accident last week and lost all her left wing primary feathers and cannot fly. She was found lying stunned at the side of the road by young Gordon, who picked her up and, as we were away, took her home and looked after her for us. When we got back he brought her along tucked inside his shirt on his bicycle. As she could not fly up to the dovecote we made a special box for her and fixed it on a post a few feet from the ground and put a plank up to the entrance so that she could walk home at bed time. We wondered whether she would have enough sense to use it and were glad to find that she had.

It means, of course, that we have to shut her up each night so that she is safe from the cat who hangs about round here at night and I imagine we will have to go on doing it for some time; I have no idea how long primary feathers take to grow. The wonder is that they grow at all. When I cleared them off the bank where they had been scattered when torn off, I could not help thinking what marvellous pieces of engineering they are. They must be far the strongest pieces of construction for their weight that are to be found anywhere in the world.

The War Against Mammalia

The cold is holding things back and, unpleasant though it is, it is not unwelcome. I read the other day in some gardening notes that the jobs to be done in March mostly consist of doing the jobs that had not been done in February. So far as this small garden is concerned it is sound advice but should include the things that have been left undone in January as well. A further spell of hard weather, therefore, gives one a little more time in which to procrastinate before the rush starts.

The lighter mornings and the indefinable look in the hedges and fields and water meadows all show that nature is pushing her way irresistibly through the winter. One feels that it is only a short time now before we emerge once more into the glory of an English spring and one only has to look very closely and listen very carefully to have it confirmed.

Snowdrops are at their best and this year seem better than ever. I believe that in our case this is because, in spite of expert opinion that cutting them down immediately after they have flowered does no harm, I left them last year until their leaves turned yellow. I also followed a tip given me by Mr Corral our butcher, who told me to spread a good dose of bone meal in October over the ground where they lived. Between the two the result has been splendid and given us and, we hope, others, for they can be seen from the road, great pleasure.

Crocuses too seem more prolific than usual, although they had to go without bone meal. It may be that the dodge of planting the new bulbs with flakes of naphthalene has paid dividends and kept the mice at bay. Certainly there are many more than usual, the yellow ones mostly out and the other colours just beginning.

To the pleasure of looking at them dotting the grass bank is added the smug satisfaction of having inflicted a defeat on the mice. The moles too seem to be momentarily contained since the arrival of a new consignment of arms in the form of traps. Rabbits, however, continue their guerrilla tactics all too successfully, but it looks as if myxamotosis will once more defeat them as it has already infected those living in the fields not far off.

The desultory campaign against the water voles, who immediately attack any kingcups that I plant along the river bank, continues lethargically, but, as they are amusing little creatures and almost as pretty to watch as kingcups, I have not the inclination to press home a really vigorous attack. One wishes so much that one could have both.

I have therefore cause to be reasonably satisfied with the progress of the war against mammalia, but my complacency was nearly shaken two days ago when soon after seven o'clock on a cold and frosty morning my wife, on drawing back the curtains, reported that there was a horse galloping about the garden. I am proud to report that as a veteran of the mammalian campaign I kept my nerve and merely asked what colour it was and drew the bedclothes a little more tightly round.

Desirable Residences

The cold and very early Easter made it difficult, and most people would have thought impossible, for the ladies of the village to decorate the church for the great day as well as they have always done it in the past. Parishioners' gardens could provide little. Our own was hardly any help and could not provide a single Daffodil; the Snowdrops and Crocuses were over and there was no blossom anywhere so far as one could see. Yet somehow or other between us all we scraped enough together to give the ladies a chance to show their skill, helped by a little cheating from Miss Child who persuaded some to ante up a bit of cash so that she could buy some flowers in Andover to help out. I happened to be at the lych gate on Saturday afternoon when three strangers, who had wandered into the church, came out and told me how lucky they had been to see our church decked out in all its glory and how splendid it looked, so it is not just local pride that makes us think what a good job the ladies did.

Though Easter Day broke cold and drizzly, it was cheered up considerably for us by the sight of a swan slowly swimming up the carrier at the bottom of our garden. We have always hoped that a pair would nest somewhere close and use our carrier, but so far none has done so. Rooks, however, have now joined the crow family in our elms and we now have five nests. In spite of the mess they make it is nice to have them about and their busy noisiness seems to become a cosy part of the surroundings. There is too the comfortable tradition that a house with a rookery is a happy one.

The rooks, like the jackdaws in another tree, are still very busy building and I have wasted a good deal of time watching them. I was much amused the other day to see the rooks, after a long session of squawking, finally reach an agreement on whatever they were discussing and they all flew away together.

Then as soon as they had all gone one of the jackdaws from a tree at the other end of the garden flew over to one of the half-finished nests and pinched a large twig from it and flew back to add it to her own.

I can quite understand the fascination of bird watching, though I would never have the patience to do it properly and certainly have not the knowledge that is required to get the full pleasure from it. We have, however, friends who stay with us at times who are very keen. In order to help them I got permission to build a small hide in the reeds opposite our house, from which they might get glimpses of some of the birds which live there, some of which, I believe, are very shy, such as certain warblers and a water rail or two.

It is an ideal place for a hide as it is on private ground and is left undisturbed from one year's end to another. I am, in fact, the only person who goes near it. I spent a good deal of time making it as comfortable as possible for our ornithological guests. It has a shelf on which they can put their cameras and field glasses and two little comfortable seats, and I even went to the trouble of lining the roof with a polythene sack so that when it rained they would be nice and dry. It is hidden behind a bush with a clear space in front and every so often I visit it and scatter a few seeds about to encourage the locals to come and help entertain our visitors.

Two of the experts are coming down next month so I thought I had better go and tidy up the place and make it ready for them. I was mortified to find that some bird had started to build her nest inside the hide itself. The nest is so advanced that I have not the heart to chuck it out, so it means that our wretched guests will now have to kneel very uncomfortably out in the open behind another bush, with rain probably pouring down their necks watching whoever she is sitting snug and dry in the hide that was never meant for her at all. It really is too bad.

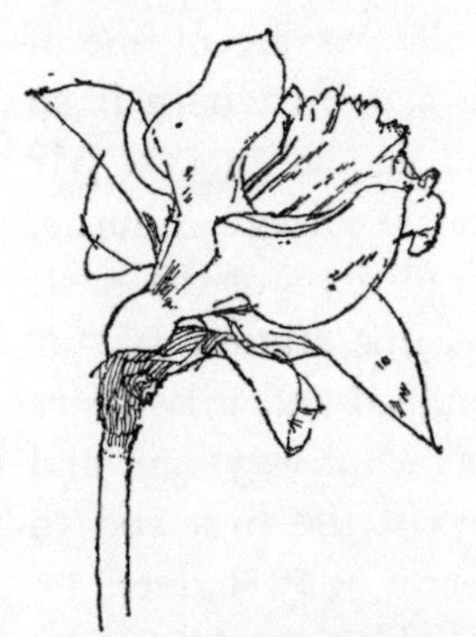

Waiting for the Spring

18th April

What a terribly late spring. Here we are in the middle of April and, but for the sight of a few hesitant Daffodils in the garden, one would hardly believe that the year is well on its way. Even these hardy plants must find the going very difficult as they try to batter their way through the morning frosts to better times, harassed and jabbed at day after day by vicious squalls of snow and sleet and hail.

The fields and hedges have hardly changed for months and the water meadows still keep the drab drear look of winter. It is difficult to find compensations. Even the most idle gardener must be getting a bit bored with it all. If one looks a bit closer, however, one can see and almost feel the pressure building up as small shoots that by rights should by now be well through begin to show and trees and shrubs cover themselves with tightly packed buds waiting for the word go.

The birds seem as impatient as the rest of us. Two days ago, when the wind backed to the south-west for a few hours, bringing soft warm rain, they all suddenly started singing as if the sun were shining and spring had arrived at last. The sound was so welcome that I stood in the rain just listening, trying to pick out the individual songs even though I could not name them. At one splendid moment I thought I heard the cuckoo far away in the distance, but I think it must have been a severe attack of wishful thinking as I never heard him again and no one has confirmed it.

The village was saddened again this week by the death of

one of its members. In a small community the passing of one of its members means so much more than in a town where it so often only affects relations and friends and acquaintances. Mr Jerret not only leaves a gap which the whole village mourns, but it breaks another link with the great traditions of the past. He and his four brothers, one of whom became station master at Waterloo, put in between them two hundred and fifty years of service with the railways. His father was a railwayman, and over a hundred years ago his grandfather cut the first sod to make the North Devon Railway. Mr Jerret may indeed be familiar to many outside the village as older readers may remember the famous Red Cross poster over twenty years ago showing him leaning out of the cab of his engine to give a coin to a small girl holding up a collecting tin.

It was always interesting to talk to him on his own subject. One realised how much more there was to know about driving an engine than any layman could guess or instruction books disclose. Where one could afford not to pick up water when one was running late; when a certain engine had to be helped and nursed over a part of the track where another of the same class could take it in her stride, and how a fireman could be saved much exhausting work and the company coal by a sympathetic understanding of one's engine and a lifetime's knowledge of the track. Mr Jerret once told me that he was always lucky with his firemen, but, listening to him, one came to realise that luck played little part.

In these days of mass production and computerised output, most men and women have not the same opportunity for developing their character in their work or personality in their skill, but it is to be hoped that the greatly increased leisure that now waits for them round the corner will allow them once more to play their part in their country as individuals. Even when long past their physical prime, they will find plenty of interesting things to do, even if it is only watching and waiting for England's spring to arrive.

Problems with Fantails and Crocodiles

2nd May

Some of the birds round our house are doing much to distract our thoughts from the weather which seems to overshadow all else.

The chaffinch and the robin, about whom I wrote earlier in the year, are now very tame. My wife rarely leaves the house without being buzzed by the chaffinch, who flies round and round her head loudly shouting for alms. His shrill persistent cries bring the robin, who always gets first pick because he is brave enough to fly up and take the offering from her hand, which Chaffy has not yet plucked up enough courage to try, though he comes within a couple of feet of doing so.

Tame robins are, of course, common. Two of our neighbours are hand-feeding theirs but we have never had a chaffinch so tame before. Until a day or two ago both the robin and the chaffinch brought their wives, who remained discreetly in the background and would never come so close as the cocks. Our friends find the same, though one of them told me that sometimes, when the cock robin has taken something from her hand, he flies off and gives it to the hen. Ours, I'm afraid, is not so gallant and the hen has to fend for herself.

A thrush has made her nest within inches of our dining-room window in quite an obvious place two feet off the ground and well within a yard of the path which is in constant use. She is now sitting tightly on four beautiful blue eggs.

The small box that I put up in a tree only last month has been occupied by a blue tit and when I looked this morning she had already laid five tiny eggs.

On the domestic front our fantails have fared less happily.

Pepper, having got bored after a week with her twins, deserted them. About a fortnight ago she decided to try again and laid two eggs, but these have now disappeared and I am pretty certain they have been stolen by one of the jackdaws. Salt, however, has made a complete recovery from her accident and has one dazzling white new wing and one grubby one and seems to be nest building, so we are hoping she will raise a family. It is rather important that she does as another pigeon has disappeared this week, probably as a result of a car accident. They insist on playing on the road and, though a near miss frightens them out of their wits for the moment, they are soon back on the road again. Unlike human beings, they seem to forget and throw off a frightening experience very easily.

I have never forgotten one of the worst frights I have ever had, though it happened over forty years ago. It was when I was working abroad. I had gone off to shoot what I could find to feed myself and the small crew of the launch in which I was travelling. I took with me as a guide an old local Mohammedan fisherman who told me that he knew where there were plenty of duck. We set off at dawn on a very misty morning and came to a small branch of the river about 100 yards wide, which we had to wade across to reach an island where the ducks were said to be.

Before we started wading, I did ask the old man whether there were any crocodiles about as I had shot one not far away a day or two before. He assured me there were not, so we started across. The water was chest high and very muddy. When we were halfway across, I heard behind me a loud sound like an explosive long drawn-out 'Pah', and a horrible fishy smell wafted across the water. I looked round and saw the dim shape of the biggest crocodile in Asia and probably in the world. It had enormous jaws full of teeth, a head about ten feet across and its body stretched away to a distance of about twenty yards until it was lost in the mist. I splashed, shouted and waded over to the island louder and quicker than I had ever waded through water before. I then addressed the old man and told him what a wicked thing it was to tell lies and that I was very annoyed by the whole incident. But I made little impression, partly because neither of us understood each other very well, and partly because he could not understand why I was making a fuss as he told me that in that district crocodiles only ate Hindoos.

As we were on an island we had of course to wade back later on and I remember wishing like the devil that I had not gone there, but we got back safely all right so the old man was probably right about the Hindoos, but I still sometimes wonder how crocodiles know the difference.

The Daffodils are in full bloom, the cherry trees are beginning to burst their buds and we heard the cuckoo for the first time last Sunday, though it was heard by others about a week earlier. The quarter's electricity bills have come through the letter box and a moorhen has started building in our carrier. If it were not for the weather one would think that spring had come at last.

Suddenly it's Summer

18th May

Suddenly it's summer. The long drawn-out winter left us without warning at the end of April, and summer, impatient as ourselves to see it go, seemed to step in suddenly and take its place while spring was still fumbling, wondering whether it were safe to appear. Temperatures leapt overnight to the seventies and kept us all hot, happy and surprised for nine heavenly days. The valley became bright green again, the air throbbed with the song of birds who came flocking in from abroad, the village cherry trees rushed overnight into full bloom and we all went round beaming and asking everyone whom we met if it were not lovely.

In days like these the country seems to leap into life and time romps by so quickly that it is impossible to keep up with it. One also finds oneself recapturing to some extent the feelings of childhood when even the most trivial incident is an exciting event. I was reminded of those times when three young people called while my wife and I were gardening, to ask if we would sponsor them for a long cross-country walk which the young people of the village were organising for charity. While we were walking round discussing the value of their stamina and the prospects of their finishing the course, we stopped at a moorhen's nest with ten eggs in it and, country children though they were, they all gazed at it with as much wonder as if none of them had ever seen a nest before, and each had to check by counting aloud the number of eggs and had to do it all over again because one of us had made it only nine.

During the recount, Gordon and Tony, who had been busy earning an honest bob clipping the grass round the posts of some wooden rails, came running at full speed across the lawn, vying with each other to be the first to tell me about their startling discovery that the bottom of one of the posts was rotten. Somehow the general excitement was infectious and for a moment or two it seemed that, whether there were ten or nine eggs in the nest and how deep the rot had penetrated, were much more important than any general election date or any of the world's unhappy affairs.

It is amazing how quickly nature, when given a few warm days, makes up for lost time at this time of year. We visited yesterday some friends whose garden a fortnight ago had scarcely a leaf or flower but is now blazing with all the old-fashioned mixture of Wallflowers, Tulips, Forget-me-Nots, Alyssum and what I am told we should now spell 'Aubrieta'. Birds too seem to be in a tremendous hurry to grow up. Part of our garden has several small thrushes flopping about with large yellow mouths and no tails and hardly any feathers under their wings. The first one I found I thought must have fallen out of his nest and I picked him up to put him back where I thought he belonged, but found the nest deserted. Nevertheless I popped him in and waited to see what would happen. Sure enough he struggled out again and went flopping off back towards where I had found him and where I suddenly noticed his mama was waiting with a worm in her beak to feed him. It must be strenuous enough feeding a hungry young family when they are all in the same nest, but it is a mystery to me how it can be done when each fledgeling is wandering round quite a large area. Yet not only is it done, but the parents find time to feed themselves as well and to sing about it all for an hour or so every dawn and also every evening, as well as at intervals during the day.

What a pity it is that humans have not the same terrific energy; the world's unhappy problems, one feels, would soon be solved, but perhaps – awful thought – they might be a great deal worse. It is probably as well, therefore, just to make the most of the glorious weather and stay still and count one's blessings and the moorhen's eggs.

Birds have a lot to put up with

6th June

We have acquired two ducks, inappropriately named Sugar and Spice as they are both astonishingly ugly. The idea (since proved false) was that they would keep down the flannel weed which has suddenly come to plague our pond. To prevent them wandering off we spent a lot of time one morning building a

cage of fruit nets to keep them in until they got used to their
new surroundings, and we spent a lot of time in the afternoon
trying to catch them and put them in again after they had got
out. In spite of all this, when finally they were allowed their
freedom they seemed to dislike flannel weed as much as we did,
much preferring some of the more precious pondside plants.

The moorhen with ten eggs managed to hatch one of them.
I saw the chick in the nest and there were then only five eggs
left. I thought the other four might have hatched but found the
smashed remains of one of them a yard of two away. Next
day, when I went to look, the nest was flattened and the
remaining eggs destroyed. As I saw no sign of the chick, I
imagined he had been destroyed as well, but three or four days
later I caught sight of him for a moment swimming at the edge
of the stream before he dodged quickly into the reeds when he
caught sight of me. I do not know who is responsible; not a
jackdaw, as the nest was flattened as if someone had pounced
on it. I strongly suspect a new and unknown cat who has
recently been wandering around spreading alarm in the
neighbourhood of the bird table where there are a number of
fledgelings still being fed by their parents.

One of the young robins now accompanies his father to the
kitchen door and waits patiently outside while my wife gives
something to his parent inside, who immediately flies out and
dutifully hands it over to his offspring. As the offspring is now
almost as big as his parent, it seems high time that he started
fending for himself. One of his brothers or sisters has already
been run over by a car, so what with cats, cars, jackdaws and
hawks, not to mention other predators, the moorhen's achievement of ten per cent production seems not so bad after all.

Jackdaws have their troubles too, but seem better able to
look after themselves. I saw one chase away a hawk the other
day who was hovering too near a nest. The hawk flew quite
slowly twice round the garden, pursued equally slowly by the
jackdaw, who kept just behind and above him until the hawk
thought better of it and, suddenly putting on a turn of speed,
returned to his usual hunting ground across the river.

Last week on his way to work, Mr Saunders saw a hawk drop something which fell at the side of the road. He found it to be a baby thrush and apparently unhurt. He picked it up and gave it to Miss Hoare, who also works in the water garden and who put it in a thrush's nest which already had young in it. She thought it unlikely that the parent birds would take to it, but that it would be worth a try. Not only did they do so, but they continued to look after it long after their own family had left the nest, and in spite of it turning out to be a missel thrush and growing as big as themselves while still hardly fledged.

One day this week Janice Simpson brought us round a swift which she had found in the road unable to fly, even when started from a height, and wanted to know what she had better do with it. Adopting my best bedside manner, I prescribed keeping the patient warm, careful nursing and a little bread and milk at intervals. I am glad to say that, inspired perhaps by her grown-up sister Eileen, who is working for her S.R.N. certificate, her nursing was such that her patient made a complete recovery.

The warm weather has brought on the soft fruit so quickly that we had to spend a lot of time yesterday morning building a cage of fruit nets to keep the birds out, and we spent a lot of time in the afternoon trying to catch them and put them back out again after they had got in. Birds are aggravating things at times, but they have a lot to put up with.

Halcyon Days

However long drawn-out last winter may have been, we are having it amply made up to us by a wonderful May and so far by a glorious June. Even when wet, May and June are magnificent months in England, but, when day after day the warm sun shines, new flowers bud and break out almost while you watch and the gardens, hedges and meadows are alive with young of all kinds, they are perfection.

Those who have the luck and health to reach an age when they no longer want to dash about doing things at top speed are indeed fortunate to live in a beautiful valley like ours and be able occasionally to sit and stare. Not that even on the most perfect day they can do it for long if they sit in their own gardens. It will be only a minute or two before their eyes light on a bunch of nettles thrusting their way through the Primulas, a plant panting for water or a box of seedlings almost hopelessly overdue for planting out.

Like most people who have gardens, we have an array of garden chairs and in our case no less than three garden seats scattered about, but the only one that is ever used is a stone one and that only by the thrushes who find it a handy anvil on which to crack their snails. The really sensible thing to do if one ever wants to sit for more than a minute or two would be to follow the example of so many of the more quick witted and hire a deckchair for the day and, with one's back to the land, spend the day gazing out to sea, happy in the knowledge that however hard one looks there will not be a weed in sight, that the waves are impossible to roll or mow and that, if one were to start watering, somebody would immediately call the police.

However little spare time one may be able to find with a

clear conscience during the day, one should certainly try and make some in the very early mornings or the late evenings, which at this time of year have a special charm. One ought, of course, to make a special effort and get up really early while the sun sucks up the dewy mist of dawn and there is a smell of freshness unknown at other times of day, but the late evenings also have their charm. Last night, shortly before ten, we strolled round our garden as the light was fading after a hot day, the air was quite still and heavy with the scent of flowers and full of the sound of scuttlings as small riverside inhabitants got ready for the night.

Even politics in these halcyon days seem locally to lack the frenzy and ebullient turbulence that one reads about in the newspapers, but it may be because we have other important things to think about.

Whether or not Mr Wilson, when settling for a general election in June, took into account that we are to hold our Church Fête on the 4th of July I do not know, but, if he is hoping that his party will win this seat, it was a fatal mistake to choose an election date so close. Not that politics are ignored. Far from it. Only this week a political meeting was held in The Peat Spade at 12.30, which was attended by our member, Admiral Morgan Giles. About a dozen of us attended and stood each other half pints, regardless of party feelings, and discussed the prospect of rain, now badly needed by the farmers. At present it is feared that none can be expected with any certainty until the day of the Fête, when for the first time for many years, if not ever, we are having a band to play on the Vicarage lawn. Happily, however, 4th July is still some time ahead, allowing us all meantime to make the most of these magnificent days.

Chemical Formula

Flannel weed is disfiguring our pond and in our particular circumstances there seems to be no cure for it.

I was told of some expert who could advise me about it and went to see him. He was a delightful man who gave me a long and learned lecture on the subject, very little of which I understood. I was, however, very glad that I went because he brought back wonderful memories of a certain Doctor Porter who had the unenviable task of trying to teach me chemistry over half a century ago.

I am glad to say that the Doctor's efforts were not entirely fruitless because I acquired at his feet a piece of scientific knowledge that has remained with me to this day, namely

> Little Johnnie's gone below
> We'll see his face no more.
> Instead of drinking H_2O
> He drank some H_2SO_4.

I remember how I always contrived to weave H_2O and H_2SO_4 into every answer to an examination paper in the forlorn hope that they might have some relevance to the question and score me a mark.

My limited knowledge of chemistry, however, never precluded me from receiving an invitation at the end of each term to attend Dr Porter's Good Boy Lecture, though I have to confess that short of being expelled and leaving no address, it was almost impossible for any of his pupils not to receive one.

The lecture was held in his class room, which held about a hundred boys sitting in horse-shoe tiers facing an enormous blackboard and a long table.

On the evening of the lecture there was placed on the table

a four-foot model of Vesuvius which was connected to a double-handed pump which was used in those days to blow up motor car tyres. Each Good Boy as he arrived surreptitiously primed Vesuvius with something varying from a mundane piece of india rubber to a small fire cracker or, by the more imaginative and scientifically minded, with a concoction specially brewed for the occasion in the laboratory.

From the roof were suspended two enormous gramophone horns, one twelve feet long and the other fourteen, to each of which a sound box was attached which played directly off a cylinder record. Dr Porter always opened the proceedings by pointing out that in spite of their size these were delicate instruments and that we must control our applause and on no account stamp our feet because the vibration made the horns jump the grooves on the records, causing not only damage to the record but discordancy in the music.

The actual lecture was dull and consisted of magic lantern slides of scenes such as the façade of the Royal Exchange or the Acropolis, enlivened at times by a snapshot of the bones of a Brontosaurus, to the accompaniment of whichever gramophone was not being wound up or having its needle changed at the time.

But at last the great moment came for which we had all been waiting – The Grand Finale. A wax record made by Dr Porter himself of his singing all four parts of God Save the Queen at the same time, was placed on the largest gramophone. A slide of a photograph of Windsor Castle taken from the roof of Eton College Chapel was flashed on the screen by the Good Boy privileged to work the lantern, who by tradition was by this time so overcome by emotion that he put it on upside down to cries of dismay from every guest.

On the terrace were three tiny black dots ('I doubt if you can see them, boys, from where you are sitting.' 'Oh yes we can, Sir.') 'Well, the figure in the centre is her Gracious Majesty the late Queen Victoria' (loud applause). The figure on Her Majesty's right is Sir Henry Ponsonby (louder applause) and the figure on Her Majesty's left (and here the

Doctor smiled bashfully and rubbed his chin in embarrassment) is me.' (Tumultuous applause and unrestrained stamping of feet, causing the horn of the gramophone to leap in the air and come down anywhere in the middle of the National Anthem and sometimes miss the record altogether.) At this point the Doctor leapt to the table and, taking off his coat, lit the Bunsen burner hidden in the bowels of Vesuvius and, with his beaming face crimson with exertion and pleasure, started pumping out its flaming and odorous contents while every Good Boy present gave him a shouted and standing ovation.

He was a tremendous character and, though his lectures were for me at any rate quite incomprehensible, we boys loved him very much, except when he made one kneel in the corner of his lecture room facing the wall while he plugged books at you at intervals in case you were not attending. But, after all, when one comes to think of it, any less kindly man would have plugged an assegai.

A Family Affair

20th July

Once again Fortune smiled on our village for the great day of our Church Fête and in spite of a gloomy forecast by the weather experts it turned out to be a lovely afternoon.

Circuses are famous for the way in which they organise their appearances and disappearances without confusion or fuss, but I suspect even they could still learn something from the parishioners of Longstock, though it is unlikely that any of those many people who work for our Fête could explain precisely how such efficiency is achieved. If seriously pressed I suspect they could only answer 'Well it's always done that way.' Tables, chairs, stalls, side shows, stoves and all that goes to make a good village Fête glide into place an hour or two before it is opened and equally smoothly disappear when all is over.

One imagines that the same table goes into exactly the same place as it always has done and the same chair into exactly the same bit of shade to be sat on by the same family that has sat on it for several generations back. Even the children, reminiscent of the prints of the cries of London, who walk round selling their wares from baskets filled with flowers and handkerchiefs and sweets and goodies and small bunches of sweet peas with lucky numbers on seem to be the same children who have sold them for years past until one looks again and realises that they are the baby sisters or even perhaps to some older inhabitants the daughters or granddaughters of the children who sold them years ago.

Our village Church Fête in short is more like a large family garden party for which many of the families have spent weeks working quietly away to make or collect things that can be sold on the day and the real secret of the efficiency and success is solid hard work.

The garden party atmosphere is greatly helped by its being held in the old fashioned garden of the Vicarage with its large lawns and magnificent shady trees, but this year it was helped even more because the committee had taken the bold and unprecedented decision of hiring a band, all the way from Bitterne, who arrived some with their wives and families and not only played extremely well but came for a specially reduced fee which could hardly have covered their expenses and which, it is said, renewed our honorary treasurer's faith in human nature which hitherto had been deemed impossible when it came to his paying out cash.

There cannot be many small villages who have such a large proportion of people willing to work so hard and efficiently to support their church and it is sad to think that this looks like

being one of the last occasions and just possibly *the* last occasion
that our Fête will be held in such happy and peaceful surroundings.

The church authorities have decided to sell the Vicarage with
its lovely garden and build a bungalow or small house nearby.
It is true that they offered not to sell it during the next ten
years if the parish were to guarantee £600 a year for that time;
but the raising of that amount every year cannot, alas, be
achieved by bowling for a pig or selling goods willingly given
and often beautifully made or small bunches of sweet peas with
lucky numbers on.

Another great event, but one that only affects us personally,
has been the arrival of a first born to Salt, our favourite pigeon.
Mother and child appear to be doing well and everyone seems
delighted – especially perhaps Sugar, one of our Muscovy
ducks, because suddenly overnight she has ceased to be the
ugliest bird in Hampshire. Salt's young hopeful looks like a
very small and very stupid vulture with an enormous beak and
a completely vacant expression. He is beginning to be covered
in white spikes instead of down and when he sits up and looks
at you he gives you quite a shock. The first time he did this I
nearly fell off the ladder but I'm getting more used to him now
and this morning when I looked into his dovecote I'm glad to
say he did not frighten me nearly so much.

Survival of the Fittest

A short time ago we went to see some friends who have a large pond in their garden which was full of tadpoles; so I asked if I might take some home because, as I have mentioned before, I have not seen a frog in our garden since we have been here. Our host found a large polythene bag about the size of a pillow case and with a saucepan we scooped up several hundreds of tadpoles into it and I emptied them into our pond as soon as we got back. They seemed pleased with their new home and swam quickly about exploring it.

I went down the next morning to see how they were getting on but all I saw were some rather smug goldfish looking it seemed to me suspiciously fat and I have not seen a tadpole since. I was therefore mildly excited yesterday, when weeding a bed near the pond, to find a very small frog about an inch long hopping about among the Primulas. It will be interesting to see if enough have survived to repopulate our little bit of the valley, which Mr Mott tells me used to have plenty of frogs not so many years ago.

I am rather afraid, however, that it will take more than a pillow-case full of tadpoles to accomplish it, as the odds against survival must be thousands to one against when one thinks of all the hazards in the shape of ducks, moorhens, snakes and so on that they have to face before they reach mature frogdom.

By the same token, during the past week I have only seen three goldfish in our pond and I am keeping an eye open now not only for small frogs but for a smug looking heron; but it may be that the other goldfish who should be there are just sleeping it off under the water lilies.

The recent rains have helped the valley to get that lush look that comes at harvest time. Most of the corn is cut and is, I am told, much better than was earlier thought likely. Certainly the uncut fields of wheat look sturdy enough and I have seen hardly any barley flattened by wind or rain.

The purple Loosestrife on the river bank is nearing its best and, when the bright plum-coloured patches of it are set off against a background of pale blue wild Forget-me-Nots, they look prettier than ever.

A walk at this time of year is well worth while and, after so much sun, a calm soft day with gentle rain in no way lessens the enjoyment. The quiet drip from the trees and the birds busily making the most of the damp earth throwing up all sorts of deliciously edible creatures and the flowers and the long grass glittering with droplets of rain all tend to make life remarkably pleasant as one travels along; but I suppose really it comes down to the state of one's liver. I have known days when sloshing along with soaking feet and the rain running down one's neck and getting an occasional wet flick in the face from a dripping bramble and ripping one's coat climbing through a barbed wire fence to avoid the foot deep mud at the gate, have been sheer misery.

I have just been watching Sugar and Spice following a hedgehog across the lawn. He evidently appeared to them to be neither edible nor dangerous and they could not make him out at all. I don't think either of them had ever seen a hedgehog before and whenever he stopped they stopped, stretching out their necks like geese to get a little closer look at him but never dared to go within two yards of him. When he finally disappeared into the hedge, they watched the spot for about a minute after he had gone, still wondering who on earth he could possibly have been.

Summer's Ripening Breath

The week or two's spell of damp and cooler weather and now back to heat again has made things grow at a tremendous rate and, though we have cut barrow loads of spent flowers from the herbaceous border, others have spread over the cleared spaces almost overnight and the bed looks as full as ever. It is difficult to keep pace with it all and also difficult to adapt oneself quickly enough to the changed conditions. After a long spell of dry heat one finds oneself still watering when it has just been raining out of sheer habit, and when the heat returns one finds oneself wondering what on earth is the new, fearsome and probably dangerous disease that has suddenly attacked so many plants causing them to wilt away almost completely. One is on the point of sending specimens in hermetically sealed envelopes to the R.H.S. for analysis when one suddenly realises that watering has once more become essential.

It is as well that we have already got back into the habit of watering as today is obviously going to be a real scorcher. The other side of the valley has that hazy look, there is the very gentlest of breezes only just moving the tops of the tall reeds and the morning air drones with the soft sound of flying bees and other insects and the occasional high-pitched whine of someone flying pretty fast. Even the cows have already sought the shade and lie under the trees twitching at the flies and just sleepily enjoying the peace of it all as well they might as they have not got to water and weed like the rest of us.

The wonderful spell of weather is going to make it a splendid year for blackberries. Last week we took a picnic lunch in the pouring rain to the New Forest and neither of us could remember seeing such great clusters of blackberries as we saw beginning to ripen where we had our lunch. Even our own garden blackberries, cultivated with loving care and pruned and dug

about and fussed over *ad nauseam*, look as if they may have a berry or two, which is a change and probably just as well as our usual limitless source of supply, which is the hedge up the lane, has been drastically cut back by our tidy-minded Borough Council.

Like many others, to judge by fairly recent correspondence in the press, I find it difficult to see why we should all have to pay extra on the rates to have the verges on the roads and lanes denuded of Cow Parsnip, Buttercups, Scabious and Dandelions, etc., and still less why we should pay to go without a free supply of blackberries.

The moorhen who nests in the carrier at the bottom of our garden has just had her nest destroyed for the third time this season, this time with six eggs in it. So far this season she has only produced one chick. I cannot find out who is responsible; obviously someone fairly large as the nests are flattened out and the eggs smashed. Nothing daunted, she has built herself another nest a few feet further up the stream and has daily laid an egg in it for the last three days. One admires her persistence. She would have a much better chance if she built her new nest fifty yards or so upstream where other moorhens seem to remain unmolested and where, as I write, one with six of her half-grown young are busy pecking away at the lawn. The young ones look so much more graceful than their parents that they almost seem a different breed of bird.

Nuisance as they are in many ways (one of their least endearing habits is pulling off the heads of water lilies just as they are beginning to flower), we would be sorry if they left us, and, taking things all round, they do not treat us as badly as some. My brother, who has a small lake in his garden, tells me that the ones he has to put up with fly up into his apple trees and peck at the apples while they are still growing on the trees, which I think must be unusual.

Return from Holiday

24th August

Like, as it seemed when we were there, ten million other people, we have been away on a visit to Ireland and came back to find soft drizzly days and summer passing peacefully away. The big elm down by the carrier has two patches of yellow where autumn has already laid her finger and blackberries are beginning to darken the hedges.

A couple of days ago house martins were swooping and diving low down over our lawn in such numbers that I went down to see what all the excitement was about, but, although I stood there for some time while many of them flew so close that they almost brushed my face as they passed, I could see no sign of a swarm of flies. This morning hundreds of them were twittering on the telephone wires discussing, one imagines, the prospects for their long journey ahead. It will not be long before they leave.

It is all too clear that we can no longer look forward this year to the excitement of new flowers, except for a few Autumn

Crocuses and our indoor Chrysanthemums which soon will have to be moved into their winter quarters in the greenhouse.

When we got back we found that our robin had finished his moulting and grown a new tail and was beginning to sing his autumn song and had completely recovered his self-assurance and friendliness. The chaffinch also had not forgotten us and started buzzing my wife once more for bits of cheese as soon as she appeared outside the kitchen. On the other hand we found that, with the exception of one (Fanny), all our pigeons had deserted us. Young Gordon, who was left in charge, told us that they gradually drifted away during our absence. One wonders what could be the reason as they had become very tame and fed out of our hands. The fact that one has remained seems to rule out the possibility of rats or hawks frightening them away. It may be that they had got so used to having us around that they felt lonely when there was no one about and went off to join some other colony. They are, after all, gregarious creatures.

We have been given four more by my brother who is suffering from a pigeon population explosion and have caged these in temporarily. It is possible that they may tempt our old ones back should they pass this way again. We very much hope so as we had grown fond of them, especially Salt whom we had nursed through her trouble with a damaged wing.

A good many goldfish had disappeared, but there is no mystery about that. The day after our return a heron flew lazily up the valley towards our pond, but on catching sight of me turned round and flew guiltily back again.

However, Sugar and Spice, our two Muscovy ducks, paddle about the same as ever and are just as friendly. They still keep their ridiculous trick of running to meet us when we appear with their breakfast and running all the way back with us to the place where we feed them down by the river. We have never fed them anywhere else, but they have never learnt to wait.

The moles, I like to think, have appreciated their respite from harassment and shown it by playing havoc with parts of the lawn; but in my inmost heart I know perfectly well that they could not care less whether I am here or in Timbuctoo for all the difference that it makes to them.

The mice, it is clear, had the time of their lives while we were away and ate half of every one of our fourteen melons, which after eight years of trying we had at last succeeded in growing.

But for all that it is nice to go away for a bit and curiously enough, in spite of what we find has been happening while we were away, nicer to come back.

The Year Grows Older

15th September

The great equinoctial gale that recently rampaged through our valley as well as through the rest of the country seems to have done comparatively little damage here but has left the countryside looking limp and exhausted. The year is too old now for things to make a quick or even, alas, a full recovery from so severe a battering. One may pick up and do what one can to help plants and bushes that fell before the wind, but they rejoin and stand bravely in the ranks again only with the help of crutches.

The storms also brought an unwelcome reminder that leaf sweeping will soon be upon us as the lawn was littered with green leaves and twigs ripped from the trees and scattered ruthlessly over so wide an area that the prospect of having to sweep them up would have daunted the stoutest heart, as indeed it did the hearts of Gordon and Tony who, on the evening they came for a job to do, viewed the scene with apprehension and sudden swingeing attacks of conscience about homework left

153

undone, until I proclaimed that I thought the mowing machine would be able to cope with most of the debris.

After so generous a summer, none of us has any right to complain about the weather, especially as at this time of year high winds and rain are to be expected. Nevertheless it is disappointing after such a rosy long-range forecast for September given out by the meteorological experts, who often this year have done so well.

Although the season is drawing to a close, there is still plenty of colour left, not only in the garden but in the wild. A friend from London, recently staying with us, refused to take back flowers from our garden or greenhouse but said that she would do some weeding for us instead. She came back from the garden with an armful of wild flowers and, from those that she did not take home with her, arranged for us as pretty a bowl of flowers as anyone would wish to see, made up mostly from bold red purple Loosestrife through thistles and Knapweed etc. to the delicate pinky mauve of Hemp Agrimony and some sort of mauve-headed grasses. The only non matching shade was a sprinkling of water Forget-me-Nots.

Looking at such a beautiful arrangement one wondered why we went to all the trouble of spending so much time trying to get rid of them to make room for their more fashionable and sophisticated cousins.

Snips, the Muscovy drake whom we got to keep Sugar and Spice company, has now been accepted as a member of the family by all concerned, though it has taken over three weeks to achieve this. Although Sugar fell for him in a big way from the moment he arrived, Spice would have nothing to do with him and went for him whenever he came too near and did her best to prevent Sugar from trying to make friends with him.

They have given us great pleasure. When one has them playing round one every day and can watch their ways so closely, it is fascinating to discover what markedly different characters three ducks can have. Though I know nothing about ducks, I think Muscovies must make more attractive pets than most kinds, particularly because of their endearing habit of talking to each other by nodding their heads close together and making soft little muttering sounds whenever anything unusual happens, just like people having a really good gossip. Sugar has completely won my heart with her trick of wagging her tail like a dog when she comes running up to my wife to be patted and made a fuss of, though if the truth were known it is, I fear, only excited anticipation of being given a bit of biscuit.

Stolen Fruit

1st October

The autumn has started in tremendous style, helped by the hot weather which arrived just in time to vindicate the long-range weather prophets who told us at the end of August that we might expect it.

Seldom have I seen the Virginia creeper covering the barn of Upper Manor Farmhouse blaze so magnificently in the sun as it does this year and some of it seems to have escaped across the road to the old Methodist Chapel where a patch of it glows like a bonfire in the hedge. Old Man's Beard seems to be romping away more than ever in the hedgerows and what few trees have started turning colour look unusually bright. I passed a chestnut tree on the back road to Andover two days ago whose leaves were almost the same colour as its own shiny chestnuts that had spilled from its branches and were dotting the verge below it.

From all accounts it is a good year for apples and many in the village are busy working in the orchards over at Leckford which are expected to produce something over five hundred tons of fruit. Our own two apple trees, which we put in as striplings five feet high eight years ago, have produced a magnificent crop of 0.0552 tons, not counting several windfalls which we have been unable to gather because someone, generally Snips, our Muscovy drake who has now grown to the size of a small goose, has got there first. No amount of shouting and cursing or threatening waves with a rake, spade or fork seems to make him understand that scrumping a windfall is forbidden. Snips, however, is not easily deterred and is never the soul of tact, and like a New Zealand trout lives permanently in hot water, sometimes literally as indeed happened only yesterday when he suddenly flew across while we were having tea in the garden and landed without warning on my wife's lap just as she was drinking a hot cup of tea and in an instant turned what had been a gentle domestic scene into a noisy and ugly brawl between a very startled woman and an indignant scalded duck.

In a recent letter I told of a heron eating our goldfish. Mr Debenham, the head riverkeeper, told me that a herring gull could also have taken his share. We were now, he said, the only MacFishery shop in the district as he had closed all his own branches by putting wire over his stews after he had seen the gull pick out a trout and peck its eyes out on the bank. I had often seen the gull about – in fact I see him most days sitting on the bridge over the river about two hundred yards down-stream from us – but I never suspected that he would do a thing like that, even though I had often seen a gull take a small fish from the sea. They are crafty hunters. I remember once, when anchored off a mud flat at low tide, watching one spending his time doing a little clog dance on the mud and then standing quite still until someone poked his head up through the mud to see what all the row was about. He went on doing it for two or three hours until the tide seeped in again, when he flew off contentedly replete.

In spite of the lovely weather it is time to start the melancholy business of clearing out old plants from the beds and bringing others in to the shelter of the greenhouse in preparation for winter's siege, but last night we cheered ourselves up after a day of it by ordering sweet peas for next year, taking at least an hour to choose ten half packets, so tantalisingly do seedsmen describe their wares in their catalogues. Long may they continue to do so for, although it is often true that it is better to travel hopefully than to arrive, in the case of sweet peas you always know that you are certain of a wonderful welcome at the other end whatever you choose.

The Death of Snips

19th October

A sharp frost of four degrees or 2.2 recurring Centigrade (what a bind all these modern calculations are for those who don't like doing sums) turned our Dahlias a few nights ago a muddy brown and reduced our Zinnias to tattered remnants of their former glory. It is all the more sad to have seen, not only because they had been such a glittering show of hard metallic colours, but the warm soft days that have been granted us since then would have suited them well and given us all a few more days of enjoying them before winter finally blotted them out.

Another sad day for us has been the death of Snips, a delightful little clown who, although we had only had him for two or three months, had already endeared himself with his trusting ways. He had been missing for a day, but my wife found him the next morning back in his usual place at the bottom of the garden lying down, being watched over by Spice and obviously ill.

Mrs Maidment, who since childhood has looked after chickens and ducks and dogs and tame rabbits and ferrets and all small animals that women who have been born and lived all their lives in the country find it second nature to do, prescribed castor oil in case he had eaten something that had disagreed with him. She and my wife, putting on their best bedside manners, went down with the bottle and spoon to administer the dose but it was then obvious that poor Snips was too ill to undergo such drastic treatment; so Mrs Maidment picked him up and carried him like a baby in her arms, talking to him gently while my wife made a bed in a box of shavings in the kitchen where he died a few minutes later.

I took him to the vet and await the report of the post mortem. I fear he must have picked up some poison.

Sugar, meantime, has laid eleven eggs and is sitting on them in a cleverly-hidden nest in a hole some way off the ground inside a hollow tree about two hundred yards away from her usual residence in our garden. The nest was found close to her cottage by Mrs Maidment, who in her motherly way automatically took Sugar under her metaphorical wing and is looking after her during her confinement. Meantime, Jill, Mrs Maidment's small daughter, has chosen five boys' names and six girls' names for the offspring when they arrive, which, as her mother points out, may mean complications if some of the eggs do not hatch or if the young do not conform if they do.

On the 11th October Longstock held its Harvest Festival service, when incidentally we learned during the sermon that harvest festivals are quite modern having been started by the Reverend Stephen Hawkes, the vicar of Morwenstow in Cornwall in 1843. I think that most people imagine, as I did, that they dated back to very early days of church history.

As usual the church was filled with an abundance of flowers and fruit from the gardens of the people who brought them in and who set about decorating all available space with their offerings. Even the carved rood screen had drifts of Old Man's Beard tumbling over it in as much profusion as in the hedges in the lanes outside.

The young people, who by ancient custom try to confine their decorations to the font and its steps, found that they had to spill out into the body of the church, so much did they bring, dominated by the giant pumpkin grown for the occasion by Maurice Nation.

So many were the offerings that there was a severe shortage of vases, but a huge bunch of Michaelmas Daisies looks equally magnificent in a humble bucket and all felt secretly confident that the Almighty would be every bit as pleased as if they had been arranged in a golden bowl by Constance Spry herself.

Young Love in an Autumn Landscape

26th October

I write on one of those lovely autumn days which fool one into thinking that winter is still a long way off: warm sun in a pale blue sky lighting up the golds and reds and rusty browns of the trees and hedges. Although driving a car with so much traffic about has long ceased to be a pleasure, it has at this time of year its compensations. It is now that one notices the great variety of trees and shrubs with their many different autumn colours which line our roads, and every bend brings a different scene. Some of the smaller roads round here are particularly beautiful as every now and then one turns a corner or crests a hill to find suddenly, stretching away in the distance before one, a large piece of West Hampshire glowing in its autumn glory.

And indeed at this time of year gardeners need some compensation because for them autumn is not all fun. Splendid yellow leaves shining in the sun look one thing on the trees but quite another thing when lying about in the flower beds and on the lawn; sweeping them up takes such a big slice out of the short days when there are so many other important and equally dull things to try to do before winter closes in.

Other compensations are perhaps the indoor activities which our village arranges so well during the winter season and which are now just beginning.

In the Village Hall one evening last week the recently-formed village Society of Church Friends arranged a showing of coloured photographs taken by Mr Durnford, a neighbouring farmer, depicting the progress of a grain of wheat from start to finish. Although it is possible that many of us may have seen individual photographs that are better, I should very much doubt if any has seen a collection of such superbly outstanding ones.

It says much for Mr Durnford's skill as a photographer and ability as a lecturer that, although the great majority of his audience live with the day-to-day scenes that he photographed, and many of them spend their days working on the land, his talk held us all spellbound for well over an hour and, in spite of the excellent cheese and cucumber sandwiches and cups of tea that the ladies provided when the talk had ended, we all felt sorry that it was over.

There are rumours that we are soon going to have a chance of seeing another of his series called 'A Year on the Test' in the fairly near future.

Another excitement we have to look forward to is a play by the young people, which they have now started rehearsing, to be presented about Christmas time. It is, I understand, still something of a secret so I do not like to ask too much about it, but one of the actresses has told me in confidence that she has a smashing part because at the end of it she marries a young gentleman who, I gather, is pretty smashing too. I was therefore distressed yesterday to be told that the young gentleman is likely to be given another part. However, Christmas is still two months ahead and when one is only eleven years old one may, I think, be justifiably released from vows of eternal fidelity at the end of a fortnight so I expect it will all turn out as happily in the end as the play itself.

I was told, again in confidence, this week of another unfortunate *affaire de coeur*. This time concerning a young gentleman about the same age who could not do something for me on Saturday morning because his lady love would not speak to him any more as she had fallen under the spell of some Lothario in one of the Wallops (a neighbouring village) and he had therefore arranged to go over and settle accounts with him that morning.

It seems that the paths of true love among our young people do not run smooth, but did they ever for any of us?

Drama Comes to the Valley

One sunny morning this week I looked out of my dressing-room window and saw a small disturbance among the unswept leaves lying about under the trees on the lawn. I paid no particular attention to it as my thoughts were busy elsewhere, probably about breakfast, but a minute or two later I looked again and noticed another small flurry among the leaves some few yards away from where I saw the first. This time I looked more carefully and saw that it was a cock pheasant. I watched him for a good minute or two and found his camouflage fascinating. A pheasant is, after all, a large bird and one would have thought that his brilliant colours and shiny black green head with scarlet markings and white collar would be difficult to hide, but they only add to the confusion.

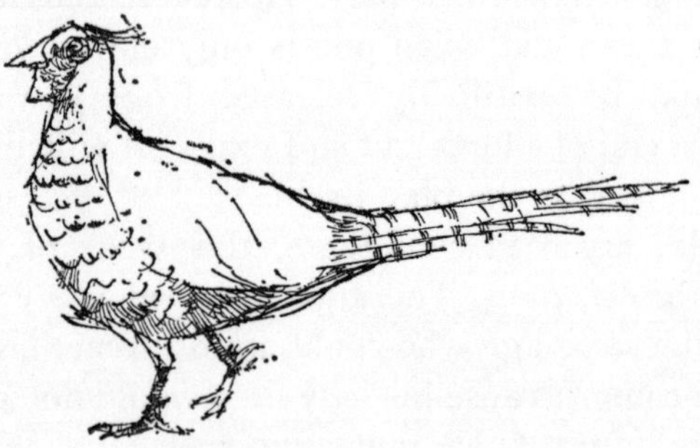

When I got downstairs he was much easier to see, though still well camouflaged. I suppose that being a ground feeder his colouring is specially designed to protect him from predators overhead such as some kind of eagle rather than from foxes or cats who are their natural enemies here.

The moorhens by contrast stood out very obviously and their black and white bobbing tails which help hide them in the reeds only draw attention to them when pecking about among the leaves.

Our tame chaffinch has come back. We had not seen or heard him for nearly a month but he suddenly turned up this week and started chinking away outside the kitchen door demanding his little bits of cheese in the same way that he always did. One wonders why he went and where he went. The hen, whom we had also not seen for some time, has returned with him so they evidently stick together.

The young people in the village played to a capacity house last week when they presented their performance of 'Puss in Slippers' by Richard Tydeman, produced by Glynis Hunt, in the Village Hall.

Described as a Panto Mini-drama, it was, as tradition demands, all in poetry, though at times some of the characters were a bit pressed for rhymes, as when the ogre, during a rather fearful and dramatic scene, was boasting his power to 'take the shape just as I wish of any kind of beast or fish', invited us to 'just say the name of any creature and I'll demonstrate before I eat you.' To the relief of all concerned, however, having demonstrated his power by turning himself into a lion, a horse, and a pig, he grew overconfident and changed himself into a rat, when, to the cheers of the audience, he was immediately disposed of by Puss. Then the Marriage Registrar who had been summoned, after he had entered the ogre's name on his 'Missing Ogres List' proceeded without delay, as instructed by Eleanor Michel who acted as compere, to declare Dacey (Maurice Nation) and Buttercup (Jill Maidment) 'to be King and Queen under rule sixteen' and so in the ringing farewell words of Eleanor Michel as the final curtain fell,

> 'We lost an ogre, gained a bride
> And done a good bit more beside,
> While in the land of Marjarine
> They're happy as a king and queen.
> The future – you can see their faces –
> Will be all Buttercups and Dacey's.'

Immediately after the performance the chairs were stacked up against the wall and the auditorium was changed as quickly as any ogre could have done it into a market where delicious home-made jams and sweets and other delectable goods were sold by members of the cast and their friends at prices which would have made any price-warring supermarkets surrender unconditionally but which nevertheless helped swell considerably the funds of the Young Church Builders of Longstock.

This week a wire fence has been stretched across the water meadows, inoffensive and hardly visible but, with the white lines that have been sensibly painted down bits of the road running through the village, one views them with sadness as being the first tiny ripples of the incoming tide of intensified commercial agriculture and urbanisation that some day will drown our valley. But perhaps I am in a gloomy and pessimistic mood. Last week I forgot to turn on the heat in our small propagating frame, with the result that many precious cuttings were lost through frost. I switched on the heat and found next day that a mouse, encouraged by the warmth, had burrowed into it and demolished the rest of the cuttings. I set a trap which caught the mouse but in the process tore out the small wire of the heater and fused it. I have now no mouse, no cuttings and no heat. I wonder how Kew and Wisley manage these things.

Quiet Dignity

Except for the sharp frost which we had a few weeks ago, we have had none until last Saturday night when for the first time this year we felt the touch of the winter ahead. Temperature remained only a few degrees above freezing all Sunday morning with a damp white mist which made it seem all the colder, with the result that there was much stamping of feet after the short open-air service round the village War Memorial by those who had been standing on the frozen grass. Although on a much smaller scale than most memorial services elsewhere, the absence of grandeur and spectacle seems almost to enhance the quiet dignity of our own, where the only piece of ceremony was when Glynis Hunt helped a small four-year-old to lay the wreath that had been specially made for the occasion by Mrs Nation from evergreens from her garden.

Whoever chose and sited our memorial could not have chosen better. The tall grey stone cross standing among small bunches of Chrysanthemums and Poppies with seven little wooden crosses stuck in the grass at its foot, reminding us of the seven villagers who left to fight and never came home again, cannot fail to stir the emotions of any who lived through the fateful years of the two great wars of our time.

The dustmen's strike fortunately passed us by, partly, perhaps, because we are blessed with a crew of men who are friendly souls and who told us that they did not want to strike, and partly because their leaders and those in power at the Head Office of the Trades Union Council may have been frightened that their efforts might be thwarted by some of the younger members of our village who had decided to hold this year on the fifth of November the bonfire of all time and who were ready to seize every opportunity to collect any combustible material that might be left lying around. Even a fortnight ago a deputation arrived to ask if it might borrow our wheelbarrow to help carry seven enormous worn out lorry tyres that someone had given for the occasion. As our wheelbarrow is made of iron I felt that it was reasonably safe to do so but nothing would have induced me to have lent our old one which was made of wood.

We were in fact away for Guy Fawkes night but I understand that the bonfire made in a field down by the river came well up to everybody's expectations. So much so that I was invited, when we returned two days afterwards, to go and view the ashes which were said to be still warm. I declined on the grounds that at my age the excitement of viewing two-day-old ashes of a bonfire, especially if they were still warm, might be too much for me, an excuse which luckily appeared to be thought reasonable.

Sugar's attempt to raise a family has failed. Her eggs, though fertile, failed to hatch. It is probably as well. Two ducks are really about all our small garden can take. Eleven ducklings would, I suspect, seriously upset the balance of nature. On the other hand, the two pigeons who hatched at the end of September are now grown up and are indistinguishable at a distance from their parents. It takes just on six weeks for them to become self-supporting from the time they hatch.

The Last Blooms of Summer

7th December

I remarked the other day that the birds seemed exceptionally noisy for this time of year and put it down to the very mild weather that we have been lucky enough to have had so far this autumn. I then remembered that two years ago I thought exactly the same thing, so it is obviously not so uncommon as one thinks. Nevertheless it is unexpectedly pleasant to hear so much bird song at this time, and every now and then listening to a thrush or chaffinch singing almost as loudly and long as if it were spring.

The garden too still shows quite a bit of life and I counted this morning quite a number of survivors from the summer – Roses, some bits of Veronica and a number of Pansies still carrying on gamely even after many months of continuous flowering. Winter Jasmine, Viburnam Fragrans and Anemones one expects, of course, to see but a Wallflower in bloom and others in bud and an occasional Aubretia flower were a surprise and made one look forward eagerly to spring again.

Our Viburnam Fragrans is better than it has ever been allowed before to be by the birds, and I think this is probably because this year for the first time I remembered to spray it with bird repellent; a new kind which I saw advertised and which seems to have been effective. I wish now that I had had more faith in it and had used it more thoroughly, but the price of the tin was so horrific that I felt at the time that I was spraying with pure gold and so fell between the stools of aesthetic plenty and financial bankruptcy. The result is a poor showing of blossom but so much better than in previous years when we had almost none. It is such a lovely bush when in full flower that I shall spray it properly next year and go to prison for debt with a happy heart.

In spite of the mild weather the chaffinch, thrush and robin, our faithful trio of kitchen door hangers-on, are growing more friendly as, I suppose, natural supplies grow more difficult to find. None, not even the robin, who we think is the son of the one who remained with us last year, yet takes food from my wife's hand, but they line up very close while all their relations and friends wait expectantly round the bird table some yards away.

Our pigeons also vary greatly in character. There are three who are much less shy than the others, although all are treated equally and have mostly been with us for the same length of time. Even the two ducks, who are sisters from the same clutch and have always been together, are quite different in character. Sugar will readily take food from anyone's hand but Spice will rarely summon up enough courage to do so and then only from my wife's, but will always go for Sugar fiercely when she sees her being hand fed.

Poor Sugar seems to be one of those who go through life being put upon by others. One day last week she got mobbed by three seagulls for no apparent reason, a thing that one feels no seagull would ever dare try on with Spice. Spice also monopolises for herself the whole of the duck house where there is room for half a dozen others, and never allows Sugar to share it, and yet they seem to be the best of friends and waddle about the garden all day happily together with, so far as one can see, hardly ever a cross word.

A Quick Change of Name

20th December

This must be one of the mildest autumns we have had for a very long time. So far we have had hardly any frost, with the result that the ground must still be quite warm. The grass on the lawn has certainly grown a lot since it was last mown at the beginning of November and really needs mowing again, but (a) it is too wet, (b) the mowing machine is away being overhauled, and (c) I am hanged if I am going to start mowing lawns in December at my time of life.

Neighbours call bearing strange tales of Aubretia and

Forsythia in flower and Crocuses in bud and Snowdrops in full bloom. An acquaintance who lives too far away for me to check went so far as to tell me, when I spoke of these things, that he had daffodils out and apple trees in bud, but this I suspect was just a bit of show off. Luckily I prevented myself from telling him about my Sunflowers coming into bud as I was told afterwards, by someone who knew him well, that he is the sort of chap who would have called my bluff. As it was I contented myself with merely looking politely patronising, which I was glad to see obviously shook him and made him wonder a bit.

We now seem to have acquired a swan. There are, of course, a large number of swans about round here and the river in front of us often has as many as twenty or so swimming about looking very handsome. They are all wild and only very occasionally have we seen one use the carrier at the bottom of our garden. The other day, however, there was such a one and, when she saw my wife come down the garden steps to feed our ducks, she left the carrier and walked across the lawn to meet her and without hesitation walked right up to her and took food from her hand. Thereafter she came regularly for five days at the same time and then deserted us. We saw her often about in the water meadows, never mixing with the other swans but keeping strictly to herself. Yesterday she came back and again today, so we are hoping she is going to join us all.

When she first arrived we rather feebly called her Edgar, but when we had stopped rolling about the floor with laughter we pulled ourselves together and changed it to Edgar Allan Poe. This quickly led to complications as my wife and I both belong to a generation which was taught that it is impertinent, if not downright rude, to call new acquaintances immediately by their Christian names. Mr Poe seemed an inelegant name for such an elegant bird, even when we explained to others that it was Poe with an 'e'. To drop the more formal Mister for the more friendly Poe seemed to make matters worse, so we decided to conform to modern practice and jump to Christian names after all, and Allan he became. Closer acquaintance, however, revealed that Allan was a she, so we hastily changed it to Ellen and tried to pretend to her and to others that we had called her that all along.

We wonder what her history has been. I suspect that she is a widow as swans are faithful creatures and I read somewhere that if they lose their mate they never mate again. I suspect also that she comes from the Thames or somewhere where she is used to people feeding her as she has no fear of us and, when feeling a little peckish, walks right up and, stretching her neck up high, hisses in our ears that it is time for a little something. Our ducks, pigeons and moorhens all accept her without question and even Spice, who is usually rather querulous and with whom one does not take liberties lightly, limited her objection to a feeble little squawk when Ellen walked right over her and put her huge grey webbed foot in the middle of her back when doing so.

The Year's End

30th December

Winter has come at last. A biting north-east wind arrived on Christmas Eve, heralding the first white Christmas we have had for many years and making our valley look magnificent in the snow and sun on Christmas morning.

A covering of snow during the night makes going round the garden the next morning very interesting. One sees all the tracks of those who use it. I was, for instance, never quite certain how many rabbits we had and am glad to see that apparently there is only one. I was even more glad to see that he did not come from the field where I suspected there might be a warren building up again.

There were tracks of a cat who had obviously been very intent about something as its footmarks were in a dead straight line across the lawn for about sixty yards after leaving the neighbourhood of the bird table, no doubt a fruitful hunting ground at night for mice seeking remnants of food. It did not seem to be interested in either the dovecote or the duck house as the marks went on straight through the hedge where they disappeared.

Spice's early-morning stroll stood out very clearly; straight from the duck house to an apple tree which she circled twice and then across our herbacious border to where she was waiting for us to bring her breakfast. Dozens of small footprints, of course, which would take an expert to distinguish, and one with a trailing tail. I wondered who it could be as the prints were much too small for a pheasant and, though it was in a wagtail's territory, a wagtail seems to me to carry his tail too high to leave a mark.

In spite of the cold and snow there was a goodly turn out for our usual carol service on Sunday evening where we all let ourselves go. There is something very pleasant about an evening service in the winter. One in particular has always stuck in my memory which was held here two or three, or it may be four, years ago. (Time these days goes so quickly that it is difficult to remember exactly when.) It was a wild stormy winter's night with a gale blowing, which every now and then sent a flurry of rain rattling against the stained glass windows. Little wisps of wind, escaping from the gale outside, came wriggling through cracks in the big east window and played round the altar candles making them dance and splutter and sometimes almost blew them out, but the gentle words of the Nunc Dimittis, sung to Foster's beautiful chant, made the small church seem remarkably peaceful and comforting and it was not necessary to be deeply religious or sentimental to appreciate it.

Today, the 30th December, the snow has mostly disappeared and, during a short walk round the garden, my wife and I saw in a patch of snow melting in the sun our first Snowdrops ready just in time to welcome in the New Year.

What a pity it is that human beings seem so often to make such a hash of a lovely world.

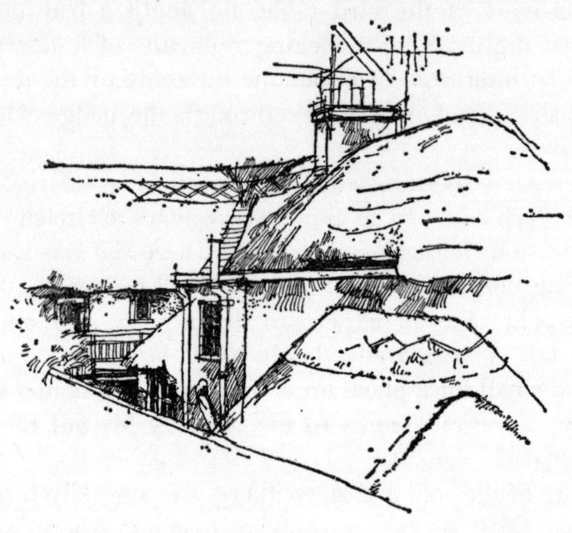

The contents of this book have previously
been published in The Gazette of the
John Lewis Partnership.